Knowing Jesus...Knowing Joy!

Are you hungry for joy in your life?

(A study of Philippians)

Find out how this special letter encourages all who read it to **know Jesus and know joy!**

MELANIE NEWTON

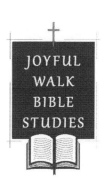

We extend our heartfelt thanks to the many women who served as contributors to this study guide, especially Liz Church, Lori Schweers, Phyllis Neal and Penny Semmelbeck. Without your help, we would never have accomplished this monumental task in a timely manner. Thanks also to the many women who served as editors for this study.

© 2016 Melanie Newton

All rights reserved. No portion of this book may be reproduced in any form without permission from the publisher, except as permitted by U.S. copyright law.

For questions about the use of this study guide, please visit www.melanienewton.com to contact us.

Cover design and study layout by Melanie Newton. Cover graphic adapted from "Jumping for joy.jpg" graphic, a public domain online image.

Published by Joyful Walk Ministries.

> *Scripture quotations unless otherwise noted are taken from the Holy Bible, New International Version ®, NIV ®. Copyright © 1973, 1978, 1984, 2011 by International Bible Society. Used by permission of Zondervan Publishing Company. All rights reserved.*

Melanie Newton is a Lifestyle Disciplemaking speaker, author, and trainer with Joyful Walk Ministries. She is the author of *Graceful Beginnings* books for anyone new to the Bible and *Joyful Walk Bible Studies* for growing Christians. Melanie can be contacted at melanienewton.com.

We pray that you and your group will find *Knowing Jesus…Knowing Joy!* a resource that God will use to strengthen you in your faith walk with God.

JOYFUL WALK PRESS
Flower Mound, TX

MELANIE NEWTON

Melanie Newton is a Louisiana girl who made the choice to follow Jesus while attending LSU. She and her husband Ron married and moved to Texas for him to attend Dallas Theological Seminary. They stayed in Texas where Ron led a wilderness camping ministry for troubled youth for many years. Ron now helps corporations with their challenging employees and is the author of the top-rated business book, *No Jerks on the Job*.

Melanie jumped into raising three Texas-born children and serving in ministry to women at her church. Through the years, the Lord has given her opportunity to do Bible teaching and to write grace-based Bible studies for women that are now available from her website (melanienewton.com) and on Bible.org. *Graceful Beginnings* books are for anyone new to the Bible. *Joyful Walk Bible Studies* are for maturing Christians.

Melanie is currently a disciplemaking trainer with Joyful Walk Ministries. She equips and encouraging Christian women everywhere to pursue a lifestyle of disciplemaking. Her heart's desire is to encourage you to have a joyful relationship with Jesus Christ so you are willing to share that experience with others around you.

"Jesus took hold of me in 1972, and I've been on this great adventure ever since. My life is a gift of God, full of blessings in the midst of difficult challenges. The more I've learned and experienced God's absolutely amazing grace, the more I've discovered my faith walk to be a joyful one. I'm still seeking that joyful walk every day…"

Melanie

OTHER BIBLE STUDIES BY MELANIE NEWTON

Graceful Beginnings Series books for new-to-the-Bible Christians:

A Fresh Start
Painting the Portrait of Jesus
The God You Can Know
Grace Overflowing
The Walk from Fear to Faith

Joyful Walk Bible Studies for growing Christians:

Graceful Living: The Essentials of Living a Grace-Based Christian Life
7 Cs of a Firm Foundation: A Study Based on Genesis 1-11
Everyday Women, Ever Faithful God: Old Testament Women
Profiles of Perseverance: Old Testament Men
Live Out His Love: New Testament Women
Radical Acts: Adventure with the Spirit from the Book of Acts
Knowing Jesus, Knowing Joy: A Study of Philippians
Healthy Living: A Study of Colossians
Adorn Yourself with Godliness: A Study of 1 Timothy and Titus
Perspective: A Study of 1 and 2 Thessalonians
To Be Found Faithful: A Study of 2 Timothy

Find these and more resources for your spiritual growth at melanienewton.com.

Contents

INTRODUCTION

Using This Study Guide 1

Introduction: ABCs of Philippians 3

Paul's Letter to the Philippians (NIV) 5

LESSONS

Lesson One: Overview 9

    KNOWING JESUS…KNOWING JOY! 11

Lesson Two: Joy in Loving Others 15

Lesson Three: Joy in Difficult Times 19

Lesson Four: Joyous Perspective 23

Lesson Five: Joy in Unity 27

    SERVING JESUS THROUGH SERVING ONE ANOTHER 30

Lesson Six: An Attitude of Joy 35

Lesson Seven: Joy in Serving Others 39

    BLESSED FEMALE RELATIONSHIPS 42

Lesson Eight: Joyful Freedom 47

Lesson Nine: Joy of Pressing On 51

    PRESSING ON TO THE GOAL 54

Lesson Ten: Joy—Firm Yet Gentle 57

    SERVING ONE ANOTHER THROUGH CONFLICT 61

Lesson Eleven: Joyful Thinking 65

Lesson Twelve: Joyful Living and Giving 69

Using This Study Guide

This study guide consists of 12 lessons. Each lesson begins by asking you to read the whole Bible passage for the lesson in one sitting to get the "big picture." If you cannot do the entire lesson one week, please read the Bible passage being covered.

THE BASIC STUDY

Each lesson includes core questions covering the passage narrative. These core questions will take you through the process of inductive Bible study—observation, interpretation, and application. The process is more easily understood in the context of answering these questions:

- What does the passage say? *(Observation: what's actually there)*
- What does it mean? *(Interpretation: the author's intended meaning)*
- How does this apply to me today? *(Application: making it personal)* **Your Joy Journey** questions are the application questions in this study. These lead you to introspection and application of a specific truth to your life.

STUDY ENHANCEMENTS

Deeper Discoveries (optional): Embedded within the sections are *optional* questions for research of subjects we don't have time to cover adequately in the lessons or contain information that significantly enhance the basic study. If you are meeting with a small group, your leader may give you the opportunity to share your "discoveries."

Study Aids: To aid in proper interpretation and application of the study, six additional study aids are located where appropriate in the lesson:

- Historical Insights
- Scriptural Insights
- From the Greek (definitions of Greek words)
- Focus on the Meaning
- Think About It (thoughtful reflection)

Two translations of the Bible were primarily used in the writing of this study. Whenever a word is followed by "NAS," it means that the word was taken from the New American Standard Bible translation. "NIV" is listed after words used by the New International Version of the Bible.

NEW TESTAMENT SUMMARY

The New Testament opens with the births of John and Jesus. About 30 years later, John challenged the Jews to indicate their repentance (turning from sin and toward God) by submitting to water baptism—a familiar Old Testament practice used for repentance as well as when a Gentile converted to Judaism (to be washed clean of idolatry).

Jesus, God's incarnate Son, publicly showed the world what God is like and taught His perfect ways for 3 – 3½ years. After preparing 12 disciples to continue Christ's earthly work, He died voluntarily on a cross for mankind's sin, rose from the dead, and returned to heaven. The account of His earthly life is recorded in 4 books known as the Gospels (the biblical books of Matthew, Mark, Luke and John named after the compiler of each account).

After Jesus' return to heaven, the followers of Christ were then empowered by the Holy Spirit and spread God's salvation message among the Jews, a number of whom believed in Christ. The apostle Paul and others carried the good news to the Gentiles during 3 missionary journeys (much of this recorded in the book of Acts). Paul wrote 13 New Testament letters to churches & individuals (Romans through Philemon). The section in our Bible from Hebrews to Jude contains 8 additional letters penned by five men, including two apostles (Peter and John) and two of Jesus' half-brothers (James and Jude). The author of Hebrews is unknown. The apostle John also recorded Revelation, which summarizes God's final program for the world. The Bible ends as it began—with a new, sinless creation.

DISCUSSION GROUP GUIDELINES

1. **Attend consistently** whether your lesson is done or not. You'll learn from the other women, and they want to get to know you.

2. **Set aside time** to work through the study questions. The goal of Bible study is to **get to know** Jesus. He will change your life.

3. **Share your insights** from your personal study time. As you spend time in the Bible, Jesus will teach you truth through His Spirit inside you.

4. **Respect each other's insights**. Listen thoughtfully. Encourage each other as you interact. Refrain from dominating the discussion if you have a tendency to be talkative. ☺

5. **Celebrate our unity** in Christ. Avoid bringing up controversial subjects such as politics, divisive issues, and denominational differences.

6. **Maintain confidentiality.** Remember that anything shared during the group time is not to leave the **group** (unless permission is granted by the one sharing).

7. **Pray for one another** as sisters in Christ.

8. **Get to know the women** in your group. Please do not use your small group members for solicitation purposes for home businesses, though.

Enjoy your Joyful Walk Bible Study!

Introduction: ABCs of Philippians

AUTHOR

Paul identifies himself as the author of this letter written to the church at Philippi, a city in Macedonia. Paul, whose Hebrew name was Saul, was born in Tarsus, a major Roman city on the coast of southeast Asia Minor. Tarsus was the center for the tent making industry, which may have influenced Paul to choose that craft as his occupation (his primary paying profession). His religious profession was that of a Jewish Pharisee.

Paul was from the tribe of Benjamin (Philippians 3:5) and trained at the feet of Gamaliel (Acts 22:3), a well-respected rabbi of the day. He was an ardent persecutor of the early church (Philippians 3:6, Acts 8:3, 22:4-5, 26:9-11) until his life changing conversion to Christianity (Acts 9:1-31, Galatians 1:11-24).

After believing in Jesus Christ as his Savior, Paul was called by God to take the gospel to the Gentiles (Acts 9:15). This was an amazing about-face for a committed Pharisee like Paul who ordinarily would have nothing to do with Gentiles (Acts 10:28). Paul wrote 13 epistles in the New Testament. Tradition has it that Paul was beheaded shortly after he wrote 2 Timothy in 67 AD. (Information adapted from *The Woman's Study Bible*, p. 1834)

BACKGROUND

Philippi was a city in eastern Macedonia, or modern northern Greece, 10 miles inland from the Aegean Sea. The city was founded in 356 BC by the Macedonian king, Philip, who was the father of Alexander the Great. Philippi was a great strategic city in the Greek empire as it was surrounded by mountains and close to the sea. Much traffic to Rome from the east went through Philippi, which served as a gateway city to Greece and Italy (a major crossroad on the Egnatian Way – one of the empire's interstates linking the Aegean and Adriatic Seas). Philippi was a transplanted Roman colony. The citizens in the colony were given the same rights and privileges as those who lived in Italy. They were able to maintain their own senate and magistrates and were not subject to regional government. Most importantly, this excluded them from taxation. Luke refers to Philippi as a "leading city of the district of Macedonia, a Roman colony" (Acts 16:12). Philippi was also Luke's hometown.

The church at Philippi was founded around 51 AD during Paul's second missionary journey (for complete story see Acts 16:9-40). During this visit to Philippi, Paul and Silas probably looked for a synagogue to share the gospel with the local Jews (as was their custom when entering a city – Acts 16:13). The lack of a synagogue indicated that there were few Jews in Philippi (as it took 10 Jewish men to start a synagogue). Paul and Silas found, instead, a group of women outside the city gates by the riverbank gathered for prayer. One of the women at the riverside that day was Lydia, a prominent businesswoman who worshipped the God of Israel (she was probably not Jewish by birth). When she heard the good news of Christ she immediately received salvation and converted to Christianity. The good news of Christ was also embraced by her household, which possibly included her servants and children. Lydia became the first believer in Philippi and was a gracious hostess to the first church in Europe, which met in her home.

Next Paul and his companions met a demon-possessed slave girl (Acts 16:16). Paul commanded the spirit to leave the girl and she, too, became a convert. Since her fortune-telling skills had been used by her owners to make a profit, they became angry with Paul for destroying their source of income. The dishonest men had Paul and Silas brutally beaten and thrown into the local jail for "throwing the city into confusion" (Acts 16:20).

While in jail, Paul and Silas met the Philippian jailer. After Paul and Silas' chains had been miraculously broken during an earthquake, the jailer who had been guarding Paul and Silas converted to Christianity (Acts 16:23-34) and his entire household believed in God and were baptized. When Paul and Silas left Philippi, Luke remained there to continue the ministry to the newly formed church. At the end of Paul's third missionary trip, Paul visited Philippi again. Paul had a very close relationship with the Philippian church. They were a source of encouragement to him and they also provided financially for his ministry more than once (Philippians 4:15 & 16, 2 Corinthians 11:9). Paul calls this church his "joy and crown" (Philippians 4:1).

Context

The letter to the Philippians was written by Paul around 61 or 62 AD during his house arrest in Rome (for details of his arrest and imprisonment see Acts 21:27 through Acts 28). Being under "house arrest", Paul was chained to a Roman soldier 24 hours a day, but was free to receive visitors and write (Acts 28:17-31). The guard was changed every 6 hours, which gave Paul an excellent opportunity to share his faith with many different guards. During this time period Paul wrote the prison epistles (letters): Ephesians, Philippians, Colossians, and Philemon. Philippians was the last letter Paul wrote from the Roman prison, as Philippians 1:21-28 seems to indicate a decision about his fate would be made soon.

Is It Happiness or Joy?

Paul's letter to the Philippians is a well-crafted expression of gratitude and joy. So, what exactly is joy? How does joy differ from happiness? Happiness is a fleeting emotion based on **external circumstances**. But true joy is different – it is something that comes from within – it's a deep abiding peace and sense of contentment and strength that is due to something **internal.**

True joy is based on a saving relationship with God and in maintaining fellowship with Him. The believer's joy is found in the inner work of the Holy Spirit. Even non-believers in Jesus can know happiness as they find it in the good things that God has given to all human beings so generously. The Christian knows a heightened joy that is rooted in the bond that exists between the believer and the Lord and the bond that exists with other believers whom we have come to love (as in Philippians 1:4, 25-26; 2:2, 29; 4:1). The deeper our relationship with Jesus and with His people the greater the joy that awaits us and the less that joy is dependent on external circumstances.

> "In the Old Testament joy is cast in terms of the worshiping community's response to God. A relationship with God was the key. In the New Testament, the most common use of joy (Greek — chairo) indicates both a state of joy and that which brings us joy. Our relationship with Jesus, particularly abiding in Him and being obedient to Him, is a source of joy (John 15:10-11). Joy is produced in us by the Holy Spirit and is a fruit of His presence (Galatians 5:22; 1 Thessalonians 1:6). It is not linked with material possessions, but rather is an overflow of salvation (Acts 8:8; 16:34). Joy is not dependent on external circumstances and is applied to suffering as well as to salvation (Acts 13:50-52; 2 Corinthians 7:4; James 1:2; 1 Peter 1:6-7)." (Adapted from *The Teacher's Commentary*, p. 934)

Paul mentions joy or rejoicing 15 times in this letter so it is an excellent mii-study of joy. That means that on average joy or rejoicing appears every 7 verses. This is even more significant when you realize that while Paul is writing these words of joy he is in prison in Rome and chained to a Roman guard! What does Paul know about joy that transcends his circumstances? Are you hungry for joy in your life? This special letter encourages all who read it to **know Jesus and know joy**!

"Joy is not the absence of trouble, but the presence of Christ." (William Vander Haven)

Paul's Letter to the Philippians (NIV)

Paul and Timothy, servants of **CHRIST** Jesus, to all the saints in **CHRIST** Jesus at Philippi, together with the overseers and deacons: Grace and peace to you from God our Father and the Lord Jesus **CHRIST**.

I thank my God every time I remember you. In all my prayers for all of you, I always pray with **JOY** because of your partnership in the gospel from the first day until now, being confident of this, that he who began a good work in you will carry it on to completion until the day of **CHRIST** Jesus.

It is right for me to feel this way about all of you, since I have you in my heart; for whether I am in chains or defending and confirming the gospel, all of you share in God's grace with me. God can testify how I long for all of you with the affection of **CHRIST** Jesus.

And this is my prayer that your love may abound more and more in knowledge and depth of insight, so that you may be able to discern what is best and may be pure and blameless until the day of **CHRIST**, filled with the fruit of righteousness that comes through Jesus **CHRIST** —to the glory and praise of God.

Now I want you to know, brothers, that what has happened to me has really served to advance the gospel. As a result, it has become clear throughout the whole palace guard and to everyone else that I am in chains for **CHRIST**. Because of my chains, most of the brothers in the Lord have been encouraged to speak the word of God more courageously and fearlessly.

It is true that some preach **CHRIST** out of envy and rivalry, but others out of goodwill. The latter do so in love, knowing that I am put here for the defense of the gospel. The former preach **CHRIST** out of selfish ambition, not sincerely, supposing that they can stir up trouble for me while I am in chains. But what does it matter? The important thing is that in every way, whether from false motives or true, **CHRIST** is preached. And because of this I **REJOICE**.

Yes, and I will continue to **REJOICE**, for I know that through your prayers and the help given by the Spirit of Jesus **CHRIST**, what has happened to me will turn out for my deliverance. I eagerly expect and hope that I will in no way be ashamed, but will have sufficient courage so that now as always **CHRIST** will be exalted in my body, whether by life or by death. For to me, to live is **CHRIST** and to die is gain. If I am to go on living in the body, this will mean fruitful labor for me. Yet what shall I choose? I do not know! I am torn between the two: I desire to depart and be with **CHRIST**, which is better by far; but it is more necessary for you that I remain in the body. Convinced of this, I know that I will remain, and I will continue with all of you for your progress and **JOY** in the faith, so that through my being with you again your **JOY** in **CHRIST** Jesus will overflow on account of me.

Whatever happens, conduct yourselves in a manner worthy of the gospel of **CHRIST**. Then, whether I come and see you or only hear about you in my absence, I will know that you stand firm in *one spirit,* contending as *one man* for the faith of the gospel without being frightened in any way by those who oppose you. This is a sign to them that they will be destroyed, but that you will be saved —and that by God. For it has been granted to you on behalf of **CHRIST** not only to believe on him, but also to suffer for him, since you are going through the same struggle you saw I had, and now hear that I still have.

If you have any encouragement from being *united* with **CHRIST**, if any comfort from his love, if any fellowship with the Spirit, if any tenderness and compassion, then make my **JOY** complete by being *like-minded*, having the *same love*, being *one in spirit and purpose*. Do nothing out of selfish ambition or vain conceit, but in humility consider others better than yourselves. Each of you should look not only to your own interests, but also to the interests of others.

Your attitude should be the same as that of **CHRIST** Jesus: Who, being in very nature God, did not consider equality with God something to be grasped, but made himself nothing, taking the very nature of a servant, being made in human likeness. And being found in appearance as a man, he humbled himself and became obedient to death — even death on a cross! Therefore, God exalted him to the highest place and gave him the name that is above every name, that at the name of Jesus every knee should bow, in heaven and on earth and under the earth, and every tongue confess that Jesus **CHRIST** is Lord, to the glory of God the Father.

Therefore, my dear friends, as you have always obeyed —not only in my presence, but now much more in my absence —continue to work out your salvation with fear and trembling, for it is God who works in you to will and to act according to his good purpose.

Do everything without complaining or arguing, so that you may become blameless and pure, children of God without fault in a crooked and depraved generation, in which you shine like stars in the universe as you hold out the word of life—in order that I may boast on the day of **CHRIST** that I did not run or labor for nothing. But even if I am being poured out like a drink offering on the sacrifice and service coming from your faith, I am **GLAD** and **REJOICE** with all of you. So you too should be **GLAD** and **REJOICE** with me.

I hope in the Lord Jesus to send Timothy to you soon, that I also may be cheered when I receive news about you. I have no one else like him, who takes a genuine interest in your welfare. For everyone looks out for his own interests, not those of Jesus **CHRIST**. But you know that Timothy has proved himself, because as a son with his father he has served with me in the work of the gospel. I hope, therefore, to send him as soon as I see how things go with me. And I am confident in the Lord that I myself will come soon.

But I think it is necessary to send back to you Epaphroditus, my brother, fellow worker and fellow soldier, who is also your messenger, whom you sent to take care of my needs. For he longs for all of you and is distressed because you heard he was ill. Indeed, he was ill, and almost died. But God had mercy on him, and not on him only but also on me, to spare me sorrow upon sorrow. Therefore, I am all the more eager to send him, so that when you see him again you may be **GLAD** and I may have less anxiety. Welcome him in the Lord with great **JOY**, and honor men like him, because he almost died for the work of **CHRIST**, risking his life to make up for the help you could not give me.

Finally, my brothers, **REJOICE** in the Lord! It is no trouble for me to write the same things to you again, and it is a safeguard for you.

Watch out for those dogs, those men who do evil, those mutilators of the flesh. For it is we who are the circumcision, we who worship by the Spirit of God, who glory in **CHRIST** Jesus, and who put no confidence in the flesh — though I myself have reasons for such confidence.

If anyone else thinks he has reasons to put confidence in the flesh, I have more: circumcised on the eighth day, of the people of Israel, of the tribe of Benjamin, a Hebrew of Hebrews; in regard to the law, a Pharisee; as for zeal, persecuting the church; as for legalistic righteousness, faultless.

But whatever was to my profit I now consider loss for the sake of **CHRIST**. What is more, I consider everything a loss compared to the surpassing greatness of knowing **CHRIST** Jesus my Lord, for whose sake I have lost all things. I consider them rubbish, that I may gain **CHRIST**

and be found in him, not having a righteousness of my own that comes from the law, but that which is through faith in **CHRIST** —the righteousness that comes from God and is by faith. I want to know **CHRIST** and the power of his resurrection and the fellowship of sharing in his sufferings, becoming like him in his death, and so, somehow, to attain to the resurrection from the dead.

Not that I have already obtained all this, or have already been made perfect, but I press on to take hold of that for which **CHRIST** Jesus took hold of me. Brothers, I do not consider myself yet to have taken hold of it. But one thing I do: Forgetting what is behind and straining toward what is ahead, I press on toward the goal to win the prize for which God has called me heavenward in **CHRIST** Jesus.

All of us who are mature should take such a view of things. And if on some point you think differently, that too God will make clear to you. Only let us live up to what we have already attained.

Join with others in following my example, brothers, and take note of those who live according to the pattern we gave you. For, as I have often told you before and now say again even with tears, many live as enemies of the cross of **CHRIST**. Their destiny is destruction, their god is their stomach, and their glory is in their shame. Their mind is on earthly things. But our citizenship is in heaven. And we eagerly await a Savior from there, the Lord Jesus **CHRIST**, who, by the power that enables him to bring everything under his control, will transform our lowly bodies so that they will be like his glorious body.

Therefore, my brothers, you whom I love and long for, my **JOY** and crown, that is how you should stand firm in the Lord, dear friends!

I plead with Euodia and I plead with Syntyche *to **agree with each other** in* the Lord. Yes, and I ask you, loyal yokefellow, help these women who have contended at my side in the cause of the gospel, along with Clement and the rest of my fellow workers, whose names are in the book of life.

REJOICE in the Lord always. I will say it again **REJOICE**! Let your gentleness be evident to all. The Lord is near. Do not be anxious about anything, but in everything, by prayer and petition, with thanksgiving, present your requests to God. And the peace of God, which transcends all understanding, will guard your hearts and your minds in **CHRIST** Jesus.

Finally, brothers, whatever is true, whatever is noble, whatever is right, whatever is pure, whatever is lovely, whatever is admirable —if anything is excellent or praiseworthy —think about such things. Whatever you have learned or received or heard from me, or seen in me —put it into practice. And the God of peace will be with you.

I **REJOICE** greatly in the Lord that at last you have renewed your concern for me. Indeed, you have been concerned, but you had no opportunity to show it. I am not saying this because I am in need, for I have learned to be content whatever the circumstances. I know what it is to be in need, and I know what it is to have plenty. I have learned the secret of being content in any and every situation, whether well fed or hungry, whether living in plenty or in want. I can do everything through him who gives me strength.

Yet it was good of you to share in my troubles. Moreover, as you Philippians know, in the early days of your acquaintance with the gospel, when I set out from Macedonia, not one church shared with me in the matter of giving and receiving, except you only; for even when I was in Thessalonica, you sent me aid again and again when I was in need. Not that I am looking for a gift, but I am looking for what may be credited to your account. I have received full payment and even more; I am amply supplied, now that I have received from Epaphroditus the gifts you sent. They are a fragrant offering, an acceptable sacrifice, pleasing to God. And my God will meet all your needs according to his glorious riches in **CHRIST** Jesus.

To our God and Father be glory for ever and ever. Amen.

Greet all the saints in **CHRIST** Jesus. The brothers who are with me send greetings. All the saints send you greetings, especially those who belong to Caesar's household. The grace of the Lord Jesus **CHRIST** be with your spirit. Amen.

Paul and Timothy

Lesson One: Overview

The Letter

This overview lesson will involve more reading and time devoted to the text than the other lessons in the study. But, reading through the entire letter of Philippians (only 4 chapters long in our Bible form) is the best way to see the entire message and get the "big picture" before we divide it into smaller pieces to enjoy it more slowly. For your convenience, the letter to the Philippians is provided for you on the preceding pages.

1. Read the letter to the Philippians as it was intended ... a letter from one dear friend to another...read at one sitting.

2. Read the letter a second time. As you read the letter this time, notice the highlighted words and phrases also listed below that represent common themes in the letter.
   - "Joy", "rejoice(d)(s)", and "glad"
   - "Christ" or "Christ Jesus"
   - References to unity (i.e.: <u>one</u> mind, same, united, harmony, etc.).
   - "gospel"

3. How often does Paul express joy in his letter?

4. How often does Paul mention Jesus Christ?

5. How often is unity emphasized?

6. How often does the word "gospel" occur?

7. What other common themes do you observe?

8. What do you learn about the Philippians?

9. What do you learn about Jesus Christ?

10. What do you learn about Paul?

11. Now read the letter again as if it were written directly to you, because it is!! (Romans 15:4, 2 Timothy 3:16) What is Paul specifically teaching you *today*?

Read "Knowing Jesus...Knowing Joy!" on the next page for additional insight into applying this lesson.

Knowing Jesus…Knowing Joy!

By Lori Schweers

What is the difference between happiness and joy? Happiness is a fleeting emotion based on ***external circumstances***. But true joy is different – it is something that comes from within – it's a deep abiding peace and sense of contentment and strength that is due to something ***internal.***

The book of Philippians is an excellent mini-study of joy. Paul mentions joy or rejoicing 15 times in this letter. That means that on average joy or rejoicing appears every 7 verses. This is even more significant when you realize that while Paul is writing these words of joy he is in prison in Rome and chained to a Roman guard! What does Paul know about joy that transcends his circumstances?

The little letter to the Philippians was written by the apostle Paul around late 61-62 AD. Paul would have been around 60 years old and he would have been a believer in Jesus Christ for approximately 25 years (give or take). Paul wrote this letter from Rome while he was under house arrest. House-arrest meant that he lived in his own rented quarters and was free to have visitors come and go and was able to freely share the gospel with all who came. However, he was chained to a member of the elite Roman guard that changed every 4-6 hours.

Philippi is located in Macedonia or what we know as northern Greece in a flat, wide valley on a small river surrounded by mountains. There was a range of mountains that separated it from the Aegean Sea and the seaport of Neapolis, where Paul first landed in Europe. The ancient name was ***Krenides*** meaning "wells" or "little fountains." In 350 BC, the name was changed to Philippi by Philip II of Macedon (the father of Alexander the Great). On an historic note: Philippi is where Marc Antony and Octavian fought and defeated the men who killed Julius Caesar (Brutus and Cassius) around 42 BC. Later Octavian became Caesar Augustus. Augustus made Philippi a Roman colony and gave Antony's army veterans land there with big farms attached. This was a smart military move as it made Philippi like a fortress on the outskirts of the Roman Empire with skilled soldiers ready to fight if needed. Most important though was being a Roman colony. Membership had its privileges!

1. Those born there were automatically Roman citizens. Roman citizenship was highly prized in the early 1st century.
2. They answered directly to Rome and not a provincial governor – less bureaucracy.
3. They had the right to appeal to the emperor (which Paul does and that's why he is in Rome awaiting trial).
4. They were protected under Roman law against punishment, execution or torture without trial (this is key when we see what Paul endures in Philippi in Acts 16).
5. ***Most important and best of all***: they paid no taxes!

This elevated status and wealth gave them pride that often bordered on arrogance. Since Paul came from a Roman colony, he understood their civic pride about their Roman citizenship. Paul appealed to this pride in the way he addresses their citizenship in Phil. 1:27 and 3:20-21 when he reminds the Philippians that their TRUE citizenship was in HEAVEN and not the Roman empire.

In Acts 16, Luke refers to Philippi as a leading city in Macedonia. This is an interesting comment since Thessalonica was the capital of Macedonia. The reason for this is that Philippi was a Roman colony and Thessalonica was not, which gave it more status. There was also a school of medicine in Philippi and some think that Luke may have attended there. But we don't know for sure.

Philippi was a bustling commercial center located on the Egnatian Way. This was a major ancient highway that liked the Adriatic and Aegean Sea. Travelers to Rome would cross the Adriatic and then continue up to Rome. Thus, Philippi was a gateway to the east.

We know that at the end of Acts 15 Paul tells Barnabas, "Let's revisit the churches we've started." They have a disagreement over who should come along and they part ways. At this point Paul takes Silas and travels to Syria and Cilicia. They then meet young Timothy who now will accompany them. In Acts 16:6, we read about Paul waiting on God to tell him where to go next. Vs. 9 describes a night vision Paul has of a man of Macedonia appealing to him to "come over to Macedonia and help us." Vs. 10 tells us that they (including Luke) left Troas immediately and departed for Macedonia. Some say this was the greatest crossing ever because the gospel was finally coming to Europe (and therefore to us). Mentioned in verses 11-13 is the "place of prayer." Why? Philippi was predominately Gentile. It took 10 male heads of households to start a synagogue. Normally when Paul and his traveling companions would enter a city they would go on the Sabbath to the synagogue to bring/share the gospel with the local Jews. Since a synagogue was not there, we can rightly assume there weren't many Jews. So Paul and his companions went where Jews typically would gather for prayer when a local synagogue was not available – the river.

Now we meet our cast of characters in the Philippian story! (Read verses 14-15). **Lydia:** She was a prominent businesswoman who sold purple cloth. Purple cloth was very valuable and worn as a sign of nobility or royalty. It was a favorite color of the Romans. She was most likely wealthy. She must have had a large home as she invited Paul's whole gang to stay. We notice that God opened her heart to receive the gospel and she responded by accepting Jesus and JOYFULLY opening her home to serve others.

Next we meet a **slave girl** who was demon possessed. She was being used for fortune telling purposes to bring profit to her disreputable masters. In verse 18, she is healed of the demon possession thereby infuriating the owners who now will lose their source of income. The charge these men made was primarily prejudicial – anti-Semitic. According to the *Bible Knowledge Commentary,* "Rome permitted the peoples of its colonies to have their own religions but not to proselytize Roman citizens. The civil leaders could not distinguish between Judaism and Christianity...." Luke was probably Gentile and Timothy was half Greek, so they weren't considered part of the "Jewish" group. These deceptive men seize Paul and Silas and have them beaten severely. Remember, this is a big "no-no" for Roman citizens. Vs. 22 says they were beaten with rods. These were wooden poles bound together and carried by the magistrates. They were then thrown in jail.

Next we meet our next convert to the gospel and member of the Philippian church. Vs. 23 mentions a **jailer** who was commanded to guard Paul and Silas securely. The jailer imposes his version of maximum security. He takes the men to the heart of the prison (the inner prison/innermost cell) and fastens their feet in stocks. So here's Paul and Silas who had committed NO CRIME – beaten and put in stocks designed to hold the most dangerous prisoners in absolute security! But Paul and Silas **chose** by an act of their will to **praise and worship God** and not let their circumstances steal their joy

Then something miraculous happens – a great earthquake occurs (vs. 26-28). To us the jailer acts rashly and threatens to kill himself, but in reality he would have been personally responsible for the prisoners and possibly would have been executed for allowing them to escape. Paul immediately speaks up, "We are all here." By this he means not just he and Silas but ALL the prisoners! Why would prisoners not have fled as soon as the doors were opened? They must have wanted to know more about this God Paul and Silas were singing so joyfully about. Joy is contagious!

Verses 30-31 are some of the most often heard: "Sirs what must I do to be saved?" Great question with a simple answer: "Believe." Believe on the Lord Jesus and you will be saved. What caused the jailer to *rejoice greatly*? He now *knew Jesus and could know joy!*

Next we see Paul and Silas being released (though the Bible doesn't say exactly why). The jailer releases them, but Paul doesn't go without a final word. He references the unfair beating they received and of course the city officials then wanted them to leave quietly realizing that they had treated Roman citizens improperly. Paul may have done this to take some heat off the new church there. Remember, if they are associated with a "trouble maker Jew" like Paul, they could also be potentially harassed. Vs. 40 – Paul and Silas once more return to Lydia's to encourage the new church before departing. From the word, "they", we gather that Luke remained in Philippi with the new church.

Paul visited these believers again at the end of his 3rd missionary journey. This was a church very dear to Paul. His love for them and their love for him are evident throughout the letter. Paul says he "longs for them with affection" and "has them in his heart." He calls them "brethren" and "beloved" as well as his "joy and crown. There is a genuine bond between these dear people and Paul and we can see that over and over in his words to them.

When Paul was arrested in Jerusalem, the church lost sight of him for 2 years. They finally heard he was in Rome in prison. While he was there they collected a gift for him and sent it along with Epaphroditus.

A sense of joy pervades the Bible. In the Old Testament joy is seen in worshiping and praising God. It was seen as the enthusiastic response of the worshiping community. It's seen as the people remember who God is and what He has done for them in the past. It's rooted in hope and confidence of what He will do in the future. A relationship is key.

In the New Testament we find joy that is independent of our circumstances. Joy can be experienced by the believer even in trials and persecution. Where does this joy come from?

- William Vander Haven said: "Joy is not the absence of trouble, but the presence of Christ." **Knowing Jesus** – think about the Philippian jailer. He believed and rejoiced. Over and over in Acts as the gospel is taken to the people and received by the people; their salvation brought an overflow of joy. Paul uses the word "gospel" an amazing 9 times in Philippians. There must be a connection between the good news of knowing Jesus and true joy.

- Jesus spoke in John 15 of the necessity of a **dependent relationship on Him** because apart from Him we can do nothing. Then he says in vs. 11 (read) that a dependent relationship and obedience to Jesus brings us HIS joy – FULL joy.

- Galatians 5:22 says that joy is produced in us by the **Holy Spirit** and is a **fruit of His presence**. Jesus said back in John 15:8 that when we abide in Him God is glorified and we bear much fruit. Again the key to joy is a dependent relationship on Jesus. Do you see why Paul says, "I can do all things through Christ?"

- Joy is most often linked in the NT with God's work in **fellow believers** whom we love and whom we serve. Many times in Philippians (as with other letters) Paul refers to the believers he writes to as his joy or considers it joy to pray for them. He rejoices in serving them and in them serving him and each other. Think of Lydia who upon receiving the gospel joyfully served as gracious host to Paul and his companions as well as to the entire Philippian church that met in her home. The jailer who received the gospel and began to joyfully serve Paul and Silas. The entire Philippian church that received the gospel and continued to joyfully serve Paul with their prayers and gifts. Of course we can't overlook Paul who wrote this joyful letter. Paul who was chained to a Roman guard but because of his deep, abiding dependency and relationship with Jesus he was able to joyfully see God working despite difficult situations. Joy in knowing Jesus is contagious. It wells up within us and motivates us to serve others in love.

Paul's focus is key. He never says, "rejoice because" or "rejoice in your pain and difficulties." He always says, "rejoice IN the Lord." The focus is on our living Lord, the one who promises to complete His work in us. The one who supplies our every need. The one who gave Himself up for us on the cross. The one who gives us the motivation and the power to serve Him with joy. The one who strengthens us in every circumstance. The one who causes us to be content. The one who supplies our every need from His glorious riches. The one whom we can know in a personal relationship. The one who longs to produce joy in our lives.

Do you know Jesus? If you don't you can **never** know true joy. Do you know Him but feel like you have lost the joy? Draw closer to Him – abide in Him – get to know Him better so He can make your joy full and complete. The German philosopher Friedrich Nietzsche said scornfully about Christians of his day, "I would believe in their salvation if they looked a little more like people who have been saved." Jesus paid for your sins on the cross so you could have eternal life and have it more abundantly. That in and of itself is enough to be joyful about and to rejoice in the Lord regardless of anything going on in your life. G.K. Chesterton says, "Joy is the gigantic secret of the Christian." I would say, it's no secret – because you **can** know Jesus and know joy.

Lesson Two: Joy in Loving Others

Philippians 1:1-11

1. Read Philippians 1:1-11. How do Paul and Timothy describe themselves in verse one?

   Think About It: "Don't you find it amazing that a great leader like the apostle Paul and his right-hand man, Timothy, chose to evaluate and describe themselves as "servants" of Jesus Christ? The Greek word Paul uses for "servant" was *doulos*, which refers to a slave who had no will, no rights, and no possessions of his or her own. Instead, he was the possession of another…forever! A slave's role in life was singular: to obey his or her master's will quickly, quietly, and without question." (Elizabeth George, *Experiencing God's Peace*, p.20)

2. ***Your Joy Journey:***

   - When you introduce yourself to others, how do you describe yourself? Or, put another way, what are the top 3 or 4 words you usually use to tell people who you are?

   - Do you think the words you choose to describe yourself reflect what is most important to you? Explain your answer.

3. To whom was the letter of Philippians addressed? Notice the words used in verse 1.

   From the Greek: The word "saint" here literally means "holy ones" or "set apart ones," and refers to anyone who is a believer in Jesus Christ. (Acts 9:13,32; 1 Corinthians 1:2; Ephesians 1:1)

4. In Philippians 1:2, Paul writes of two spiritual blessings he desires to impart to the readers by writing this letter. What are these?

5. Read verses 3-8 again, taking time to think about and meditate upon the words Paul chose to express what was on his heart. How would you describe Paul's attitude and feelings toward the people of the church of Philippi from these verses?

6. *Your Joy Journey:* Describe the relationships in which you participate or partner in God's service, as Paul describes here.

7. Look again at Philippians 1:6. Having "confidence" in someone or something is wonderful.
   - Using a dictionary, define confidence.

   - What are the reasons Paul gives in verse 6 for his confidence concerning the saints in Philippi?

8. Reading again and taking time to reflect upon Philippians 1:6, what do you learn (or are reminded) about the character of God?

9. How can having confidence in God, that is, the assurance of His willingness and His power to complete (NIV) or perfect (NAS) His good work in our lives and in the lives of people we love, help to bring us contentment and joy? Explain your answer.

LESSON TWO

10. How could a lack of confidence in God (and His willingness or ability to work in people's lives) rob someone of joy?

11. Reading Philippians 1:9-11 again, what is Paul's first prayer request for the Philippians?

12. What are the two qualities he desires for them in this request?

13. Why are each of these qualities important in a Christian's life?

14. What is the end result, for which Paul prays?

15. **Your Joy Journey:** Are you moved to pray any differently for your loved ones, after looking more deeply at Paul's prayer here? Explain.

16. Twice in this passage Paul uses the phrase the "day of Christ Jesus." Simply put, the "day of Christ Jesus" refers to the day when Jesus will return. (Luke 17:24-37, 1 Corinthians 1:4-9, and 1 Thessalonians 4:13-18 contain references to this event if you wish to read further about it.) What did Jesus Himself say about this day? Look up John 14:1-3 and note what Jesus promised His followers.

17. ***Your Joy Journey:*** In the busyness and distractions of daily life, do you find yourself forgetting to remember that Jesus promised that He would return someday? How might recalling to mind that Jesus is coming again bring joy to your life?

18. ***Your Joy Journey:*** Looking back over Philippians 1:1-11, which one thought most brings joy to your heart? Explain your answer.

Lesson Three: Joy in Difficult Times

Philippians 1:12-18

> ***Historical Insight:*** How did Paul end up in chains in a Roman prison? While he was visiting Jerusalem, some Jews had him arrested for preaching the Good News, but he appealed to Caesar to hear his case (Acts 21:15-25:12). He was then escorted by soldiers to Rome, where he was placed under house arrest while awaiting trial- not a trial for breaking civil law, but for proclaiming the Good News of Christ. At that time, the Roman authorities did not consider this to be a serious charge. A few years later, however, Rome would take a different view of Christianity and make every effort to stamp it out of existence. (*Life Application Bible Studies, Philippians and Colossians*, p. 5)

1. Read Philippians 1:12-18. As in most letters, Paul tells what is going on in his life. What did Paul say were his "circumstances"?

> ***Scriptural Insight:*** In contrast to the situation in Philippians 1:15-17, Paul describes preachers in Galatians 1:6-9 who are preaching a different gospel than the true gospel of Jesus Christ. Paul's response to this situation is that he hopes that the preacher who distorts God's truth is "accursed" or that his message be destroyed. See also 1 Corinthians 15:3,4 and 1 John 5:10-12 for the essential elements of the true gospel.

2. What are at least three results of Paul's circumstances?

> ***Think About It:*** Paul enjoyed a powerful personal witness to the elite Roman guard (verse 13). He was always chained to a member of the Praetorian Guard, the Imperial Guard of Rome. Every six [or perhaps four] hours his guard changed. That's 365 days a year, for two years. At [at least] four guards a day, Paul had 2,920 opportunities to share one-on-one about Jesus! Perhaps some of these soldiers who were sent throughout the Roman Empire spread the message of Jesus Christ they had heard from the lips of the prisoner Paul. What a ministry! One Paul would not have had were he not under their guard. (Elizabeth George, *Experiencing God's Peace*, p. 36)

3. In verse 12, Paul uses a term for progress (NAS) or advance (NIV) of the gospel, *"probope,"* which depicts a group of woodcutters clearing the way through an impenetrable forest for an advancing army. Why do you think this might be a good description of what is going on in this passage?

4. In Philippians 1:14 Paul states that his imprisonment made many of the other believers in the church in Rome bold in proclaiming the gospel. Why do you think this happened?

5. *Your Joy Journey:* Share an experience when the courage or circumstances of another person inspired you to do something you had desired to do previously, but had lacked the courage or willingness to do.

6. As Paul continues to describe his circumstances in this letter, he tells of two groups of teachers who are preaching the gospel of Christ in his (Paul's) absence due to imprisonment. Read Philippians 1:15-17 again. In the space below, describe each group and their differing motives in sharing the gospel.
    - Group one:

    - Group two:

7. Even though these two groups had very different motives in sharing the good news of Jesus Christ, what was most important to Paul?

8. What lessons can you learn from Paul in this situation?

9. Read Philippians 1:12-18 once more. As you read through this passage, note the many ways Paul "bloomed where he was planted"—even when he was "planted" in prison!

10. List as many of the different possible ways you can think of in which a person could respond to unfair circumstances (*i.e.:* anger, self-pity). Then think about why Paul chose to rejoice, to "bloom" where he was planted. Write down your thoughts.

> ***Think About It:*** Have you ever stopped to consider how few of the circumstances of life are really under our control? We have no control over the weather or over the traffic on the expressway or over the things other people say and do. The person whose happiness depends on ideal circumstances is going to be miserable much of the time! And yet here is the Apostle Paul in the worst of circumstances, writing a letter saturated with joy! His circumstances cannot rob him [Paul] of his joy because he is not living to enjoy circumstances, he is living to serve Jesus. (Warren Wiersbe, *Be Joyful*, P. 15,16, and 18)

11. **Your Joy Journey:** Are there circumstances in your life today that are difficult for you, to which you seem "chained," or perhaps even seem to "imprison" you? Or, has there been a time in your life when you would have said this was the way things seemed to be? Describe or draw how you felt in the space below.

12. Especially in light of your answer to the previous question, read Romans 8:28 and answer the following multiple-choice questions according to what this verse promises. Discuss your answers with your group.

    - To whom is this verse addressed?

        a. Every person who is alive and breathing
        b. Only people whose lives are successful and full of good things
        c. People who love god and are called according to his purpose
        d. Only the people to whom this letter of Romans was addressed originally

    - Do you personally qualify for this promise? (That is, do you love God and are thus called to His purpose?)

        a. Yes
        b. No
        c. I'm not sure

KNOWING JESUS…KNOWING JOY!

- What is God's involvement in your life?
    a. God leaves me alone and doesn't know what is going on in my life
    b. God knows what's going on in my life but He doesn't care
    c. God knows but isn't powerful enough to do anything about it
    d. God cares, God knows, God is powerful, and God is actively involved in my life

- How many things (or circumstances, people, other) in our lives are included in God's purpose?
    a. Some things
    b. Only the obviously good things
    c. All things
    d. Nothing

- What are these "things", or specific circumstances, doing in our lives? (Circle as many as apply.)
    a. Working together for good
    b. Becoming part of the "big picture" of the fullness of the life God has given me
    c. Helping me better anticipate my future in heaven

13. **Your Joy Journey:** Looking back over this lesson from Philippians 1:12-18, how can the truths from God's Word help you to transform your perspective and lead you to greater trust in Jesus Christ and help you choose "to bloom" where our all-wise God plants you? (The byproduct of this transformation will be greater joy in your life.)

Lesson Four: Joyous Perspective

Philippians 1:19-30

1. Read Philippians 1:19-30. Remember that Paul is under house arrest in Rome, chained to a guard and that is the situation from which he writes this letter to the Philippians. What does Paul expect and hope will come out of his situation?

   From the Greek: The Greek word translated "deliverance" here was used in different ways in the New Testament. It often meant spiritual deliverance—salvation, being born again. Here (v. 19) Paul used the word to refer to either the final stage of his salvation (cf. Romans 5:9) or future vindication in a Roman court. It seems unlikely that he had his release in mind since in the next two sentences he wrote of the real possibility of his near death. (*The Bible Knowledge Commentary NT*, p. 651)

2. **Your Joy Journey:** Thinking for a moment about your own life, what comes first to your mind when you think of some of your most "earnest" expectations and hopes for yourself? Are they anything like Paul's? Explain your answer.

3. According to Philippians 1:19, though Paul is limited in his own abilities by his current chains, what are two elements that he knows are at work on his behalf?

4. **Your Joy Journey:** Does this help motivate and encourage you to pray differently on behalf of others? Explain your answer.

5. Read Philippians 1:21-30 again. What is Paul's great struggle/conflict in this passage?

6. What are the benefits and liabilities to each side of this struggle?

	BENEFITS	LIABILITIES

- To live:

- To die:

7. In your own words, what do you think Paul means in verse 21 when he says that "to live is Christ and to die is gain"?

8. ***Your Joy Journey:*** Taking time to meditate further upon this idea, write down two ways in which Paul's statement (verse 21) could affect your life.

> ***Think About It:*** death had no terrors for Paul. It simply meant, "departing." [See Philippians 1:23,24] Soldiers used this word; it meant, "to take down your tent and move on." What a picture of Christian death! The "tent" we live in is taken down at death, and the spirit goes home to be with Christ in heaven. (Read 2 Corinthians 5:1-8.) The sailors also used this word; it meant, "to loosen a ship and set sail." ... But departure was also a political term; it described the setting free of a prisoner. God's people are in bondage because of the limitations of the body and the temptations of the flesh, but death will free them. Or they will be freed at the return of Christ (Romans 8:18-23) if that should come first. (Warren Wiersbe, *Be Joyful*, p. 45-46)

9. ***Your Joy Journey:*** In Philippians 1:25, Paul reflects upon his own usefulness to the Philippians if he were to go on living. In your life as well, God has placed people who need you for their "progress and joy in the faith." Who do you think some of these people are in your own life, or, with whom would you like to develop this kind of a relationship? Consider using some creative means to describe this in your life (drawing, poem, song, other).

10. **Your Joy Journey:** Read Hebrews 10: 24, 25. What are some of the ways in which you currently help those around you to grow and have joy in their faith? Share your answers with your group in order to consider, encourage, and stimulate one another to love and good deeds.

11. Looking again at Philippians 1:27-30, write out three or four qualities which Paul encouraged the Philippians to continue to develop in their lives.

12. What do you think Paul means in verse 27 when he exhorts the believers to "conduct yourselves in a manner worthy of the gospel of Christ"? (See John 13:14, 15; Galatians 5:16-26; Ephesians 4:1-3 for help in answering this question.)

13. In Philippians 1:29, what has been "granted" to the saints?

14. Both of these seem to be presented as privileges. What do you learn (or are reminded of) concerning suffering from the following verses?
    - Romans 8:16-18—

    - 2 Corinthians 1:3-7—

    - 1 Peter 3:14-17—

KNOWING JESUS...KNOWING JOY!

15. ***Your Joy Journey:*** How could this kind of mindset, in your current circumstances, make a difference in your life?

Think About It: Sometimes we have unrealistic expectations of what life should be (i.e.: everyone will like me, life will always be good, I can find security in this world, etc.). The natural result of these unrealistic expectations is disappointment when we are confronted with life's realities (insult, injury, rejection). We can certainly suffer if we hold onto these unrealistic expectations, but much of this kind of suffering is unnecessary and can be corrected by biblical thinking and perspective. Jesus Himself said that in this world we will have trouble, but we can still experience joy as we trust Jesus and walk in truth day by day.

16. ***Your Joy Journey:*** What do you learn from this week's lesson that most helps to deepen your understanding of joy through living for Jesus?

Lesson Five: Joy in Unity

Philippians 2:1-11

1. Read Philippians 2:1-11. As Paul writes to his beloved church, he encourages them to be truly united in Christ. According to verse 1, what aspects of the Christian life make unity attainable?

2. Have you experienced any of these truths within the body of Christ? Select one of the above and share with your group what this means to you.

3. According to verse 2, what would make Paul's joy complete?

4. In verses 3-4, we learn that our attitude towards others affects everyone around us and directly impacts the church. Contrast the sort of mindset that hinders unity with the mindset that promotes unity?

5. In what ways do you think women in general, or you specifically, might struggle with thoughts of "selfish ambition" or "vain conceit"?

6. According to Philippians 2:5, whose attitude are we to share?

KNOWING JESUS...KNOWING JOY!

7. In verses 5-11, Paul describes the attitude of our Lord Jesus Christ as the ultimate example of humility and selfless concern for others. According to verses 6-8, who is Jesus? (See also John 10:30.)

   Scriptural Insight: The incarnation was the act of the preexistent Son of God voluntarily assuming a human body and human nature. Without ceasing to be God, he became a human being, the man called Jesus. He did not give up his deity to become human, but he set aside the right to his glory and power. (*Life Application Study Bible*)

8. How did He view His deity during His time on earth?

   Think About It: Although Jesus Christ was Himself the Creative Deity, by whom all things were made, as man He humbled Himself—set aside His divine prerogatives and walked this earth as man—a perfect demonstration of what God intended man to be—the whole personality yielded to and occupied by God for Himself. (Ian Thomas)

9. Jesus' love and concern for the human race resulted in His enduring a series of specific humiliations, culminating in a terrible death, otherwise termed His condescension. God ultimately rewarded Christ's obedience by exalting Him. Using any resources available to you, define these words:

   - Condescend:

   - Exalt:

10. In the chart below, summarize and compare Jesus' condescension and exaltation:

Jesus' Actions (vv.6-8)	Jesus' Rewards (vv.9-11)

11. Re-read Philippians 2:10-11. Also read Isaiah 45:23. How will every human being respond to the name of Jesus one day?

12. ***Your Joy Journey:*** How do **you** respond to the name of Jesus?

13. ***Your Joy Journey:*** Read Mark 10:45. Jesus' motivation for living was to serve, not to be served, and to ultimately give His life as a ransom for many. How can you more fully demonstrate the attitude of Jesus in your…?

    - Home —

    - Church —

    - Neighborhood —

14. ***Your Joy Journey:*** How do you think this week's lessons concerning unity and the attitude of humility might relate to your knowing peace and joy in your own life?

Read "Serving Jesus Through Serving One Another" on the next page for additional insight into applying this lesson.

Serving Jesus through Serving One Another

By Melanie Newton

In Philippians 2:5-11 are some of the most beautiful words ever penned. As beautiful as they are, they are not just stuck in there unrelated to the rest of the letter. They fit into the context beginning 1:27, going through chapters 2-3 up to 4:3. Paul spends the majority of his time in the rest of the letter expounding on what he means in 1:27, "Conduct yourselves in a manner worthy of the gospel of Christ and stand firm." How? In one spirit, like-minded, united, serving one another. Jesus is given as the perfect example of a servant. Jesus' example should encourage us to have servants' hearts. Not just to serve one another, but the focus should be serving Jesus through serving one another. This is stated clearly in 2 Corinthians 4:5. *For we do not preach ourselves, but Jesus Christ as Lord, and ourselves as your servants, for Jesus' sake.* That would be joyful service. This naturally leads to 3 questions: 1) who is Jesus, and why is He worthy to be served? 2) how is He the perfect example of a servant? And 3) what does it mean to serve Jesus through serving one another?

WHO IS JESUS, AND WHY IS HE WORTHY TO BE SERVED?

This, of course, is a very important question. A proper answer is essential to your faith and to mine. In our passage today, someone named Jesus is to receive worship that only belongs to God. One of the charges made against Christianity through the centuries is that we worship 3 Gods: the Father, Jesus, and the Holy Spirit. Do Christians believe in more than one God? No. Emphatically the Bible teaches that there is one God only. (See the diagram at right.)

- We believe in one God Who is Tri-Personal—in three persons.
- All three are one God; each is not the other. This is how God has revealed Himself in the Scriptures.

Jesus Christ is God in His eternal divine nature. Our passage today equates Jesus with God. Jesus Christ is truly and fully human, but without sin. The second person of our triune God took on a human nature and body when He was conceived by the Holy Spirit in the womb of Mary. So, what do Christians believe about Jesus Christ? (See diagram at right).

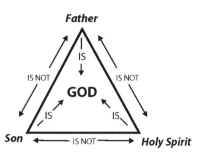

- We believe that Jesus Christ is One Person, who possesses two natures: divine and human. He is 100% God and 100% human.

In the first 200 years after Jesus' death, several heresies cropped up that lessened Jesus' deity or His humanity. Not unlike what's going on today. So, the early church came to an agreement about all of this in 325 AD at the Council of Nicea, a town in modern-day Turkey. Thus, this agreement is called the Nicene Creed. (See at end of this essay.) Since then, it has stood as an accurate representation of the Bible's teaching. At another council 125 years later, Jesus' complete divinity and humanity were confirmed. Since then, all Christian denominations—Protestant and Roman Catholic—agree on these 2 issues. God is one in essence, three in person; Jesus Christ is both fully God and fully man.

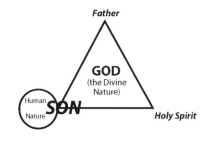

Who is Jesus, and why is He worthy to be served? He is God. Which leads us to the next big question.

HOW IS JESUS THE PERFECT EXAMPLE OF A SERVANT?

He is our perfect example because He illustrates in Himself four characteristics of a true servant.

1. Jesus thought of others before Himself.

Although God, He did not consider that high position as something that He could not give up. So, He emptied Himself, or made Himself nothing. He poured Himself out and gave Himself away. The opposite of using His divine attributes for His own advantage. Did He cease being God? No. As God, He could not and did not give up His divine attributes or nature. But, He laid aside His glory and the **independent** use of His own attributes as God. He chose to accept human limitations—the body and nature of a man—and live on earth **dependent** on the will of God the Father. He needed to do that for us, to fulfill our need. That's what the scripture says in Hebrews 2:14,17—*Since the children have flesh and blood, he too shared in their humanity so that by his death he might destroy him who holds the power of death—that is, the devil...For this reason he had to be made like his brothers in every way, in order that he might become a merciful and faithful high priest in service to God, and that he might make atonement for the sins of the people.*

2. Jesus served—He used that physical body of His to be a servant.

Philippians 2:7 describes Jesus as a servant, or more specifically, **a bondservant**—someone in bondage or servitude to someone else. Can be willing or unwilling. Jesus did not pretend to be a servant. He was not an actor playing a role. Throughout the Gospels, we see Him willingly serving others. For us women, while on earth, Jesus demonstrated that He loves women by serving them.

- He spoke to them publicly when a rabbi wouldn't even speak publicly to his wife.
- He let them support Him with their own money.
- He let women travel with Him during His public ministry. A definite no-no for rabbis.
- He let women be the first witnesses to His resurrection.
- He was sensitive toward women, performing miracles for them out of His compassion.
- He never spoke condescendingly to women, never made derogatory jokes about women, never humiliated or exploited women.

And women who know Him love Him! Right? And <u>want</u> to serve Him! Women of His day responded to His example and His love by doing the same. Did you know that a number of women traveled with Jesus, helping to support Him and His dozen hungry disciples out of their own means? We read this in Luke 8:2 and 3. They were giving of themselves, no doubt doing the laundry and some on-the-road cooking. They loved Him.

Jesus is our servant still—He is our high Priest interceding for us in prayer. We saw that in the Hebrews verses. One commentator said that doesn't mean we should be ordering Him around saying: "Fix this, or fix that."

3. Jesus sacrificed—He took that body to the cross and willingly died.

His human nature died; His divine nature didn't. He did that for us, with the joy of our redemption in mind.

4. Jesus glorified God—He humbled himself, but God raised him from the dead and exalted Him back in heaven.

Hebrews 12:2 tells us that with the joy of our redemption and His glorification set before Him, He endured the cross. And, He took back to heaven His glorified human body. Did you know that? When we see Jesus, He will still be like us! Jesus was the perfect example for us of a true and joyful servant. Now, the third question.

WHAT DOES IT MEAN TO SERVE JESUS THROUGH SERVING ONE ANOTHER?

Paul says in Phil. 2:5 that our mindset/thinking pattern should be the same as that of Jesus. We are to serve one another, as He did and does for His Body, the Church. The Church Universal as the Body of Christ is not an organization but something living. It transcends all cultures, languages, and geographic and political boundaries. Knowing we are part of this gives us radically different reasons for behaving well—reasons such as preserving and encouraging that fellowship among all believers produced by the Spirit indwelling each of us. What each of us does affect positively or negatively the other members of this organism, the universal Body of Christ represented to us in our local church body.

It's so easy to approach church as we do any other organization or business—as a consumer. We shop around for the best church with the most to offer our children and ourselves. Consumer Mentality. We come to our classes, expect childcare for our children, enjoy the fun, sometimes leave a little money, and then go on to the next shopping or activity. The Church is a living organism, not a store. God designed the Church to depend on the individual members serving one another.

How do we serve Jesus through serving one another? What is it like to be joyful servants? Let's follow Jesus' example.

1. Jesus thought of others before Himself. So, Joyful servants think of others before themselves.

We need to consider others as worthy of preferential treatment. The scripture doesn't say we are not to look out for our own interests, but only as there is equal or greater concern for the interests of others. To be a servant involves taking care of ourselves so that we can give more effectively in serving Jesus through serving others. That involves getting rest, food, exercise, recreation, a shower, and an occasional retreat. Those things benefit us. One JOY lady started a diet and exercise program for herself so she could serve Jesus with more energy. When God would call her to do something, she wanted to be physically ready to do it.

Jesus had privileges as God, reigning over the universe. But He did not consider His equality with God as *something selfishly to be held onto.* He thought of us and our needs. He did this so we didn't have to continue living selfish lives. He has enabled us to be others-oriented. All those things listed in Phil. 2:1 are ours. We have been cared for very richly so that we don't need to be thinking about ourselves all the time. We can instead concentrate on one another: serving Jesus through serving one another as He did. And, that means everyone, even those in leadership. Jesus taught that to his disciples in Matthew 20:25-28. The Church is to have a totally different mindset from that of the world. Jesus is our example in this.

2. Jesus served, so Joyful servants serve.

According to 2 Corinthians 4:5, if I am to have the mindset of a servant this is how I should think: "I yield myself to Christ to be a servant, to use what I am and have for the glory of God and the good of others." Romans 12:1 tells us to take our everyday, ordinary life—sleeping, eating, going-to-work, and walking-around-life—and place it before God as an offering. This is our spiritual act or of worship. The Greek word used there generally refers to the ones who served in the Temple, dedicated to the service of God who were **both serving God and worshiping God at the same time.** Our service is to be an extension of the worship we render to God.

A word with similar meaning but specifically applying to women is found in the Titus 2:3-5. Older women (age, maturity, experience) are to be *reverent* in their behavior. That doesn't mean to go around acting like a nun all the time. The Greek word translated *reverent* is similar to the one referring to the spiritual act of worship in Rom 12:1. We as women are priestesses serving in the temple of our God—the temple being our own bodies. God doesn't dwell in buildings anymore. He dwells in people. Therefore, there is no sacred/secular division in a woman's life. What you do at church is no more sacred service than caring for your families and homes. Everything you do is service to God within His temple—your body. If we are serving Jesus as Lord, then serving others will develop as a very natural way of life. Routine jobs around the house are no longer boring chores but instead are opportunities to serve one another in love. You are free because you are serving willingly. Like Jesus did.

> "We learn a relationship—an attitude toward life, a stance—of servitude before God, and then we are available to be of use to others in acts of service... A servant Christian is the freest person on earth!" (Eugene Peterson, *A Long Obedience in the Same Direction*, pages 66, 68)

What counts as service? First, at home, meeting the needs of your family. In I Timothy 5:10, Paul describes good works for women as including "bringing up children (not just your own but children within your sphere of influence), showing hospitality (this would include serving strangers also), washing the feet of the saints (day to day tasks at church, helping other Christians), helping those in trouble and devoting herself to all kinds of good deeds." Notice that the list covers many areas of life and practically all areas of service to the family of believers as well as to outsiders. In your daily life, you can encourage others to have Paul's perspective on life that was "to live is Christ". Do you realize that part of that includes allowing others to serve you? Let them have the joy.

The focus of serving is Jesus, not on earning favor with God or with people.

> "True service always finds its source in loving our Savior, wanting to hear His Word, and then promptly obeying. As we listen to the Lord in faith with a willing heart, he can use us and produce His fruit in us." (Cynthia Heald, *Becoming a Woman of Grace*, p. 79)

In John chapter 12 is the beautiful account of Mary of Bethany anointing Jesus with the most precious item she owned—a jar of expensive nard. Her act of service was motivated by her love for Jesus. It serves as an example to us of how to serve Jesus with our hearts. We can't serve Him physically, but we can serve Him through serving His body, the Church.

3. *Jesus sacrificed, so Joyful servants willingly sacrifice.*

Author Warren Wiersbe made this comment in his commentary on Philippians:

> "Many people are willing to serve others if it does not cost them anything. But if there is a price to pay, they suddenly lose interest. Jesus became obedient to death—even death on a cross!" (Warren Wiersbe, *Be Joyful*, p. 63)

He goes on to call this the *submissive* mind. He says that the woman with the submissive mind does not avoid sacrifice. She lives for the glory of God and the good of others; and if paying a price will honor Christ and help others, she is willing to do it. Wiersbe goes on to say that "sacrifice and service go together if service is to be true Christian ministry." That **true service costs something.** What do you think about that?

Do you realize that humans are more likely to buy into an idea that costs something? Cult leaders know that. Communists know that. When recruiting men, communists would ask someone boldly to undertake something that would cost him. The willingness to sacrifice was one of the most important factors in their success. It's what attracted and held youths in the movement as well as among extremists who advocate their cause through killing innocent people. How much greater and more beneficial is the cause of Christ! Wise Christian leaders know that sacrifice is necessary if there is going to be true growth and ministry. Service can't always be easy.

There is a difference between sacrifice and suffering. Suffering is usually imposed on you by someone else. Sacrifice is something you are willing to give. The humble mind doesn't talk about how much you sacrifice but how much you receive back from the Lord. And, you don't whine. Whining has no place in willing sacrifice. We live in a nation of complainers. Everywhere we turn we hear complaints. Joyful servants don't whine. Doing a job and then griping about it is not service.

Jane Austen, a nineteenth century author, wrote novels that were humorous commentaries on the social behaviors of her time—*Pride and Prejudice, Emma, Sense and Sensibility*, and *Persuasion*. In the latter, she draws a stark contrast between whiners and true servants in the form of three sisters. The older is haughty and doesn't even try to serve anyone else but herself. The younger sister complains continually about how she takes care of everyone else but receives no respect from anyone. Actually, she complains continually and spends more time trying to draw attention to herself than serving anyone. The middle sister Anne is the true servant, cheerfully caring for others, not drawing attention to herself. The only one experiencing joy is the one who is spending less time thinking about herself and her own needs.

Saying no to some things is okay—to be more effective in what we are doing. Some tasks or situations in a ministry need to be eliminated or changed because they are not an effective way to serve Jesus. As sisters in Christ, part of the Body of Christ, knowing how our actions affect everyone else in the Body, we need to do this the right way. There is a difference between complaining and seeing a problem and working toward a solution. (See *Serving Jesus Through Serving One Another, Part 2*.) Here's another way to think about it: "Bloom where you are planted and rejoice at what God is going to do instead of complaining about what God (or someone else) did not do." Joyful servants willingly sacrifice.

4. Jesus glorified God. So, Joyful servants glorify God.

Romans 15:1-7 is a parallel passage to today's lesson. In it, Paul exhorts believers to be patient with one another, try to please one another, accept one another, and seek unity with one another so that *"with one heart and mouth you may glorify the God and Father of Our Lord Jesus Christ."* We are living, breathing, walking, and talking representatives of the living God. We are living letters to the world around us. We are telling the truth about who God is by the way we live as well as by what we say. And, that glorifies God.

One day all will bow before Him and confess that He is Lord. Of course, it is possible for people to bow and confess today, and receive His gift of salvation. If you have never done this, now is the perfect time. Now that you know who Jesus is, you can talk to your leader about how to trust in Him.

Conclusion

Serving one another is not the main goal, serving Jesus is. The other is the means. He is our source of joy. Therefore, we can be joyful servants for Him. Serving Jesus is from the heart, not a task. Joyful servants willingly sacrifice and don't whine about it. Ask yourself: How am I serving Jesus? Try some things out to see what's a good fit. True Christian service is fun, for you. And, gives glory to Him.

Lesson Six: An Attitude of Joy

Philippians 2:12-18

1. Read Philippians 2:12-18. What does verse 12 reveal about the Philippian believers?

2. Verses 12 and 13 are one continuous thought. In verse 12, what request does Paul make of his beloved church?

Notice the terminology Paul uses in verse 12: "to work out" your salvation, not "to work for" or "work to keep" your salvation. God's grace is absolute and limitless, and the work of salvation through Jesus is complete and finished forever (see John 10:27-30 and Ephesians 1:13, 2:8,9). We did not do anything to achieve our salvation, but we must do something to exhibit it. We can put to work, or use, what God has placed in us.

3. In what ways can we work **out** our salvation in our everyday, practical living?

4. What type of attitude are we to have as we work out our salvation?

5. Explain what you think this attitude means.

6. According to verse 13, who enables us to live a life that honors God?

7. What do you think "according to His good purpose" (NIV)/ "for His good pleasure" (NAS) means?

8. Read Philippians 2:14-16 again. These verses specifically instruct us how to live out the salvation that God has worked in us. According to verse 14, what are we to avoid?

9. Why is complaining and arguing (NIV), or grumbling and disputing (NAS), so harmful in the life of a Christian and the life of the church?

10. If we don't give in to complaining and arguing, what is the result, according to verses 15-16?

11. **Your Joy Journey:** A transformed life is an effective witness to the power of God's Word. Do you think you are shining brightly in your universe, or are you clouded by complaining and arguing? Explain your answer.

12. What practical steps can you take to shine for God in a greater way?

13. In Philippians 2:17-18, Paul shows us what a life of purpose and sacrifice looks like. How does Paul view himself?

Scriptural Insight: A drink offering consisted of wine poured out on an altar as a sacrifice to God. (see Genesis 35:14; Exodus 29:41; Numbers 28:24)

14. According to Philippians 2:17-18, what is Paul's attitude toward his own personal suffering?

15. How does he encourage the Philippians to respond?

16. How do you think Paul's attitude compares with that of our modern day society in the following areas?
    - Personal suffering:

    - Living a life of sacrifice and service:

    - How a person finds joy in this life:

17. **Your Joy Journey:** Look for ways to work "out" your salvation this week (without complaining or grumbling, of course). Pray for an opportunity (or opportunities) to show God's love to other people, then share with your small group next week.

> ***Think About It:*** Even if he had to die, Paul was content, knowing that he had helped the Philippians live for Christ. When you're totally committed to serving Christ, sacrificing to build the faith of others brings a joyous reward. (*Life Application Study Bible*)

Lesson Seven: Joy in Serving Others

Philippians 2:19-30

1. Read Philippians 2:19-30. Describe Paul's relationship with the following two men:
   - Timothy (See also Acts 16:1-3; 1 Timothy 1:2; 2 Timothy 1:2-5; and 1 Corinthians 4:17)

   - Epaphroditus

2. Re-read Philippians 2:1-8. How did Timothy and Epaphroditus exhibit the attitude and mind of Christ?

3. According to Philippians 2:21, what concerns Paul about Christian believers?

4. Why do you think this is so?

5. ***Your Joy Journey:***
   - Do you think your schedule and concerns tend to crowd out your Christian interest in and service to others? Explain your answer.

   - What steps do you think you can take to remain focused on the interests of Jesus Christ?

6. Read Philippians 2:25-30. List Paul's reasons for sending Epaphroditus back to the Philippians.

7. According to verse 29, what kind of people should the church honor?

> ***Scriptural Insight:*** Paul admonishes the church to honor him [Epaphroditus] because of his sacrifice and service. Christ gets the glory, but there is nothing wrong with the servant receiving honor. (Read 1 Thessalonians 5:12-13.) There is no contradiction between Philippians 2:7 ("made Himself of no reputation") and 2:29 ("hold such in reputation"). Epaphroditus was a blessing to Paul and to his own church, and he is also a blessing to us today! He proves to us that the joyful life is the life of sacrifice and service...He and Timothy together encourage us to submit ourselves to the Lord, and to one another, in the Spirit of Christ. Christ is the Pattern we follow. *(Warren Wiersbe, Be Joyful, p. 87)*

8. How does this compare to the kind of people the world honors?

9. ***Your Joy Journey:*** Do you personally know someone who, according to Paul's standards, is worthy of honor? Share with your group, and spend some time praying for these servants of God.

Philippians 2:19-30 gives us insight into mentoring. In Paul's case, his mentoring of younger, less experienced men resulted in the blessing of sharing the workload of ministry and growing closer to the Lord together.

10. Using any sources available to you, define the word "mentor."

11. Describe how Paul was mentoring Timothy and/or Epaphroditus.

12. ***Your Joy Journey:***

- Do you have a spiritual mentor in your life right now? Or, have you had in the past? Describe the impact this person has had on your life.

- Are you currently mentoring anyone in the spiritual sense? Describe what this "mentoring" looks like?

   Think About It: If we want to impact lives as Jesus did, we will give people opportunities to grow, and then encourage them if they fail. It means taking the time to pray with them, train them, and encourage them. Sometimes it means watching them fail the first time they try a new task...Let's not let fear hold us back. Let's be more like Jesus. Let's see people as He saw them – people with great potential. (Adapted from *Becoming a Woman of Influence* by Carol Kent)

Read "Blessed Female Relationships" on the next page for more application to this lesson.

Blessed Female Relationships

By Melanie Newton

In his letter, Paul tells the Philippian believers, and us, to be likeminded, united in love for each other, one in purpose because we are already one in the Spirit. In other words, Paul is telling them "You have been united so stay that way."

He tells us we can be united when we follow Jesus' example of submission and service, when we consider others as better than ourselves and look out for their interests as well as our own. But this calls for a radical lifestyle, opposite what our culture in America teaches—me, me, me. "Don't step on my rights to pursue pleasure."

We can ask ourselves several questions to make us think about our attitudes toward ourselves and toward others in light of Christ's example.

- "In what ways do you as a woman struggle with selfish ambition or vain conceit?"
- "How do you regard one another as more important than yourself?"
- "Write your own goal and attitude for living. "I won't do...."
- "Will you voluntarily set aside your rights, status, conveniences, preferences, so that you can serve others?"

Paul says we should have the same attitude as Jesus. And, the good news is that we can have this serving attitude because God is doing the work in us. Not conjuring up on our own, we are partners with Him to get it done.

The very next sentence Paul goes for the jugular—two attitudes that get expressed verbally that can cleave unity as much as the San Andreas Fault is splitting California—grumbling and arguing.

- Grumbling springs from a bad attitude expressed in muttering, whining, & griping.
- Arguing springs from an arrogant attitude, starting as grumbling and leading to outright disputes.

You know very well that we women have a strong tendency to mutter, grumble, whine, and gripe. And our relationships often feel the brunt of our "ungrateful" and "discontented" attitudes.

Paul contrasts these attitudes with the shining examples of Timothy and Epaphroditus with whom he had such blessed relationships. No grumblings or petty jealousies. Quality relationships. Paul/Timothy — father/son; Paul/Epaphroditus — brother/brother. I couldn't help but think about our relationships as women—mother/daughter, sister/sister. We are all daughters, most of us are mothers, and we are all sisters—either by family or through Christ. And many of us are blessed with the privilege of rearing daughters.

How do we as women shine like stars among a generation of bitter, unhappy, and sometimes perverted women? How do we raise our daughters? This brings me back to a subject I did a lot of speaking on several years ago—the friendships of women. The Lord gave me some wonderful insights so I dug out my notes and pulled from them whatever was appropriate for applying today's lesson.

THE DRIVE FOR RELATIONSHIPS

We have a special gift from God, our designer, that most men don't have—a gift for relating, for caring and sharing. And so there is a drive within us to have relationships, especially close friends.

Here's an excerpt from *Anne of Green Gables* that expresses a girl's desire for a friend:

"Marilla, do you think that I shall ever have a bosom friend in Avonlea?"

"A--a what kind of a friend?"

"A bosom friend--an intimate friend, you know--a really kindred spirit to whom I can confide my inmost soul. I've dreamed of meeting her all my life.

I never really supposed I would, but so many of my loveliest dreams have come true all at once that perhaps this one will, too. Do you think it's possible?"

"Diana Barry lives over at Orchard Slope and she's about your age. She's a very nice little girl, and perhaps she will be a playmate for you when she comes home."

Anne met Diana, they pledged eternal friendship, and Anne went home the happiest girl in the world. (Anne of Green Gables by L. M. Montgomery)

Girls need friends. When young girls grow up to be women, we still need friends. God, our Creator, designed us that way. He made us to be relators so that we could respond to those around us, care for them, communicate with them, and be in tune with their needs. He even gave us an instruction manual so we would know how to best use this gift for caring and sharing. The Bible is our textbook for living. As we are discovering through JOY, it deals with every area of our lives, including what kind of friendships God desires for us to have. Throughout the scriptures, He teaches His children about being a friend and about choosing friends.

God's pattern for friendship can unleash and channel a woman's gift for caring. It makes sense that God who created us with the ability to carry babies under our hearts and nurse them tenderly at our breasts would also equip us with a longing and a skill for responding to the needs of those who are vulnerable. Yes, women have a God-given gift for intimately caring and sharing that can be used to bless the world or cruelly to ruin it for someone. From the time we are little girls, we try to surround ourselves with friends. What we learn in our girlhood influences our relationships to women as adults.

Girls and boys behave differently with their friends.

Boys may have friends over frequently, but they seem more absorbed in their activity than in each other. Men, also, do things together, usually side-by-side, engrossed in an activity, whereas women will be face-to-face.

A girl is much more likely to sit across a bed from her friend, whispering and giggling, preferably behind closed doors so their secrets cannot be overheard. They are absorbed in each other. They prefer to sleep together to continue whispering and giggling. There is usually an open show of affection between little girls, both physically like handholding but also verbally through "love-notes" that reaffirm how special each is to the other. Girls are just, generally, closer than boys.

Girls are more demanding in their friendships than boys.

They demand an intensity of closeness and loyalty. We women care a lot about our feelings for each other, and it starts in kindergarten! And when we leave our girlhood behind, we expect our women friends to share from the heart and to nurture us with expressed affection. We are disappointed when a close woman friend doesn't.

Females like to have lots of friends but still tend to feel most comfortable with a single best friend.

There is that longing for a close friend. Anne's definition was,

"A bosom friend-an intimate friend, you know-a really kindred spirit to whom I can confide my inmost soul. I've dreamed of meeting her all my life " (*Anne of Green Gables,* p. 58).

Now there is nothing wrong with longing for a best friend, but this desire for closeness and intimacy can go haywire.

Little girls and big girls are closer, yes; but, they are also crueler than boys!

Studies show that girls have a tendency to go straight for the jugular. Girls do not kick and bite, as a rule, but the verbal slings and arrows they hurl at one another and their merciless acts of vengeance are often far more painful. Two girls who are arm in arm one day will the next day suddenly turn on each other, screeching cruel insults at each other where everyone can hear. The wounds may not heal for months, maybe never. Girls have a tendency more than boys to draw a close intimate circle and leave others out, hurting them deeply and not caring!

Girls are often motivated by the desire to secure their own positions.

If a girl's needs for intimacy are being met in a friendship or in a close circle of friends, she does not want that threatened by any other person. Since the feminine identity is so closely tied to relationships, it is quite natural to want to guard our relationships by making our circle tight--even if the side effect is betrayal or cruelty. Your daughters may have experienced this already.

Or, you moms may have been the victim of this kind of hurt yourself. You know the routine:
- "They drew a circle and left me out!"
- "They formed a club and didn't invite me to join."
- A few days later that club disbanded but the next week a new secret club formed including you but excluding another brokenhearted girl.

A girl's natural, intense desire to be close almost automatically endows her with a tendency toward cruelty. Newcomers threaten her circle of two!! Girls, more than boys, are threatened by anyone who might change the relationships that give her security and self-esteem. If she needs to turn on another in order to secure her own position, she will!

Watch out for the books your little girls are reading. Some authors so effectively portray the dark side of little girls in their writings, making cruelties sound humorous, setting a pattern for gossipy, backbiting behavior, that even though there is often a 'good' ending to the book, it's too late to redeem the damage down to the young readers. Little girls do not need inspiration in the area of treachery from an adult author! What they read can seriously affect their own thinking and behavior.

Relating is a learned behavior. We learn how to relate by watching others relate to us and to each other. Moms, what kind of role models are influencing your daughters in their relationships? Do we change when we become women? Do we stop throwing darts? Do we stop chewing up one another? Hollywood doesn't believe that we do, based upon what we see on TV and in the movies.

PITFALLS OF ADULT FEMALE RELATIONSHIPS

The world of women's groups is often a refinement of the cruelty of elementary school clubs. We've become more discreet than we were as children: we choose gossip and backbiting over screeching on the playground! Some women have been so wounded by other women that they no longer pursue friendship with their own sex, denying their need and losing out on the benefits. Though we do become kinder in maturity, and certainly in Jesus Christ, we still are prone to inflict wounds on others, maybe unconsciously. What are some of the weapons used to inflict wounds?

Gossip

> "A gossip betrays a confidence, but a trustworthy man keeps a secret." (Prov. 11:13)

The Hebrew word for gossip in this verse means "traveling" with confidences. That's exactly what it is. Certainly not a communication of love, but rather, betrayal is involved, for you are sharing a secret that should have remained in your own heart. Right? Murmurings.

Why are we tempted to be faithless? Because of our strong desire for connection enjoying the spark of intimacy that gossip provides. Same thing applies to muttering and grumbling. Feel connected to the one w/whom you've shared your opinion.

> *"A perverse man stirs up dissension, and a gossip separates close friends." (Prov. 16:28)*

This Hebrew word for gossip means "to roll to pieces." This reminds me of taking crackers, putting them in a Ziploc bag, and using a rolling pin to crush them. Rolling them to pieces. If my talking is going to roll someone to pieces, then I am gossiping.

Although men do gossip, women gossip more.

Direct Verbal Assault

Not only do women use gossip but also direct verbal assault. You know what I am talking about. So does Paul—disputing/arguing. He even tells two women to stop their disputing in chapter 4. Until we can learn to find our security in Jesus Christ alone, we will have problems in this area, because we are females. We have that strong desire for connection to fill our need for security and self-esteem.

> *"Do not let any unwholesome talk come out of your mouths, but only what is helpful for building others up according to their needs, that it may benefit those who listen." (Ephesians 4:29)*

This scripture should be learned by every female from the time she can talk.

Jealousy

Then there's behavior that springs out of jealousy! Novelists often portray women as being more jealous, more backbiting, than men. Perhaps we are. Perhaps our low self-esteem makes us more vulnerable, for example, to the sin of rejoicing over another's misfortune. How unlovely! Both men and women struggle with feelings of jealousy, but women are more apt to express them.

> *In Proverbs 27:4, Solomon says: "Anger is cruel and fury overwhelming, but who can stand before jealousy?"*

If you've ever been the victim of envy, you've tasted its cruelty. Think of all the wicked characters in fairy tales — Cinderella's stepmother, Snow White and the wicked queen, and others. Their actions are motivated by envy. Envy says, "I could forgive you anything, except what you are; except that I am not what you are." Envy diminishes both parties: it hurts the victim and gives a hard and bitter spirit to the perpetrator.

> *"A heart at peace gives life to the body, but envy rots the bones." (Prov. 14:30)*

Remember the story of King Saul and Jonathan, his son, yet best friend of Saul's rival, David. Saul was the king, but he had his eye on pleasing people so he couldn't bear comparison and criticism. Jonathan was next in line but had his eye on pleasing God. He felt God's pleasure with him when he, Jonathan, exalted David.

Perhaps the key is "when we feel the intimate pleasure of God (Philippians 2:13), it doesn't matter how He chooses to work with our brothers and sisters." God is pleased when we can overcome our knee-jerk reaction of envy and rejoice with a successful friend.

So what is the answer? For one thing, we must choose friends carefully and learn how to be a good friend. Also we can't just leave our children to make friends by chance --whether it be with a neighbor, schoolmate, or other acquaintance--without any training on how to be a good friend. What happens to our daughters? Well, the natural instinct to be close is easily corrupted by the sin nature to cruel behavior of girls toward one another.

THE ANSWER

Cruel behavior can be nipped in the bud. Right now! With us as women, with our daughters, early in their lives!! Christian women and girls can be different. And they should be!! Paul says shine like stars, and we can be glow-in-the-dark stars, blameless and above reproach, shining in a world that expects women to be petty, deceiving, whiney, gossips.

What kind of star do you want to be? A brilliant white one like Polaris—how many of you have seen the North Star? For centuries men used it to find their way. Or a supernova—all show on the outside but actually a star that has disintegrated?

How do we learn to be good friends? How do we properly satisfy this desire for connection?

Let's teach these verses in Phil 2 and others like them to our daughters and stress them year after year in their relationships with other children. This girlish tendency towards cruel, teasing behavior does not have to be inevitable. It can be changed! Just as death is not natural, neither is this behavior really natural. God did not originally create women to be that way!

Through the power of the Holy Spirit who gives us Christlike attitudes (thoughts and attitudes of love) producing in us Christlike actions (words and deeds of love), that nurturing instinct can be channeled in the right direction, towards all girls with whom your daughter is acquainted. Towards all women with whom their mother is acquainted. Benefiting others. **Being a warm, nurturing Christian friend is learned behavior.**

And, moms, they learn much of their skills at relating from us. How do we treat our daughters? How do they see us treat other women? What do they hear us say in the privacy of our own home about women who are our friends, our acquaintances, our sisters in Christ, our fellow workers? Do we treat newcomers to our Bible study or women's group as outsiders? Is there an air of exclusiveness among the women of this church? If there is, and you feel it, by all means let your leader know it immediately. What does a newcomer say, a shy person, or a woman from a lonely home situation?

Okay, girls are closer than boys, girls expect a lot from their friends, and a girl's need for security in a relationship can lead her to be cruel and snubbing. Women are grownup girls with that same ability to be close, that same expectation of loyalty, and that same need for security in a relationship with at least one other woman friend. How can we properly satisfy that desire for connection?

Well, the wonderful news is that we can learn to satisfy our desire for connection through Jesus Christ because He'll teach us to be faithful and loyal. Just as glow-in-the-dark stars need to be exposed to the light in order to glow, so do we. And that light is Jesus, the light of the world, who will shine through us. We will radiate His light. Glow in the dark.

The Holy Spirit gives us brand new attitudes—**Christlike Attitudes** (faithfulness and loyalty to Him and to our sisters)—acted out in new actions—**Christlike Actions** (being faithful through our speech, saying only what helps, encourages, or blesses that person)—in order to **Benefit Others** (they are built up, encouraged, and they see God in us). Then the world sees God in us because the mark of the Christian is LOVE!!! Right?? And we will truly be as stars in the night—giving light and guiding others along the way to Jesus.

Lesson Eight: Joyful Freedom

Philippians 3:1-11

1. Read Philippians 3:1-11. What wonderful reminder does Paul give the Philippians (and us) in verse 1?

2. Who is to be the source of their (and our) joy? (Also read Psalm 32:11, Psalm 34:1-5 and Hebrews 12:2-3 to answer this question.)

> ***Think About It:*** It seems from this repeated emphasis [to rejoice in the Lord] that the Philippian Christians needed this word. Most of God's people need this challenge often. It is easy for believers to let circumstances discourage them. The cure for discouragement is to rivet one's attention on the Lord and rejoice in Him. It is significant too that a Roman prisoner would beseech people who were free to be joyful in their Savior. It seems that it should be the other way around. Paul learned what every child of God needs to learn—there can be rejoicing in the Lord even when outward circumstances are contrary to the Spirit of rejoicing. (*The Bible Knowledge Commentary New Testament,* p. 658-659)

3. The church at Philippi was made up primarily of Gentiles; they were mostly Roman citizens, and as such, did not come from a Jewish background. Explain what and whom Paul warns the Philippian believers about, based upon what he wrote in Philippians 3:2 and what the following verses address.

   - Acts 15:1-11—

   - Galatians 3:1-6—

4. In contrast, how are the people of the "true circumcision" described in Philippians 3:3?

5. Read Philippians 3:4-6 again. In verse 4 Paul says, "If anyone else has a mind to put confidence in the flesh, I far more." List four advantages he had from birth.

KNOWING JESUS...KNOWING JOY!

6. How did Paul view his privileges and achievements according to Philippians 3:7?

   Think About It: "Legalism exalts the flesh and stifles the Spirit—Liberty grounded in truth stifles the flesh and exalts the Lord." (Cynthia Heald, *Becoming A Woman of Grace*, p. 58)

7. Things are not very different today. Legalism or religious tradition can rob us of joy and freedom in Christ. We can begin to focus on ourselves and our accomplishments. But what is God interested in our doing?

   - Matthew 22:36-40—

   - Romans 13:8-10—

   - Galatians 5:22,23—

8. *Your Joy Journey:* Are there any "gains" in your life (perhaps from a time before you trusted Christ, or perhaps since you've come to know Jesus Christ) that need to be counted as loss so that you have security in Christ alone? Explain your answer.

9. Paul gained a great deal in place of his self-righteousness. Read Philippians 3: 8-11 several times...don't miss a thing!!

   - What relationship has he gained?

   - What righteousness has he gained?

   - How has he obtained this righteousness?

LESSON EIGHT

10. **Your Joy Journey:** Are these true of your life? Share when these became true for you.

11. Instead of looking for earthly applause, what new goals and new motivations has Paul gained?
    - v. 9-that I may:
    - v. 10-that I may:
    - v. 10-that I may:
    - v. 10-that I may:
    - v. 10-that I may:
    - v. 11-that I may:

12. **Your Joy Journey:** What is your fundamental goal for your life? What motivates you to reach that goal? Discuss ways you can begin to value "things" less and Christ more.

13. **Your Joy Journey:** How does this passage of Philippians deepen your security and confidence in joy through knowing Jesus?

Lesson Nine: Joy of Pressing On

Philippians 3:12-21

1. Read Philippians 3:12-21. The Greek word "perfect" in verse 12 implies a "state of completion, no more development needed." In these verses, Paul makes two admissions that he has <u>not</u> attained perfection. What have we already learned about this in Philippians 1:6 and 2:13?

2. For what purpose did Christ "take or lay hold" of Paul?

3. What was Paul's response to God's call, even though he knew he was imperfect? Refer also to Romans 7:15-8:2.

4. Look at Philippians 3:13-14. What "one thing" did Paul say is his goal? See 1 Corinthians 9:24-27 as well.

5. Forgetting in this context does not mean losing all memory of his sinful past but leaving it behind him as **done with and settled**. What did Paul need to "forget"?

   Think About It: "But one thing I do..."How would you finish this statement, dear friend? The famous preacher D. L. Moody wrote these words from a scholar named Gannett in the margin of his Bible beside Philippians 3:13: "Men may be divided into two classes—those who have a 'one thing' and those who have no 'one thing' to do; those with aim, and those without aim in their lives... The aim in life is what the backbone is to the body: without it we are invertebrate." How frightening it would be to be "invertebrate"—to be spineless, weak, and weak-willed—especially in the Christian life! But thanks be to God for these cherished-yet-instructive verses about the process whereby you and I may know and accomplish our "one thing"—attaining the great prize of the Christian race. (Elizabeth George, *Experiencing God's Peace*, p. 95)

6. ***Your Joy Journey:*** What do you need to "forget?"

7. Read Philippians 3:15-17. In Philippians 3:15, Paul uses another Greek form of the word "perfect" meaning: relative development, maturity. What do you think are some of the characteristics of a maturing Christian? (See also Hebrews 5:13-14.)

8. What part do you think perseverance plays in Christian maturity? (See also Romans 5:3-5 and James 1:2-4.)

9. How would you advise another believer to press on to Christian maturity?

10. *Your Joy Journey:* Do you think you are following your own advice? Explain.

11. Paul says in Philippians 3:17 to follow his example as he follows Christ. From the following verses, what are the advantages to those who pattern their lives after wise counselors and persevering believers?
    - Proverbs 19:20—

    - John 13:13-17—

12. *Your Joy Journey:* Now consider taking the challenge to be one who models *Christlikeness* to others. What would *Christlikeness* uniquely look like in you?

13. **Your Joy Journey:** Have you discovered an area of passionate interest in God's service yet? Explain your answer.

14. Read and re-read Philippians 3:20-21. Don't miss a thing!! Summarize these verses in your own words.

15. **Your Joy Journey:** Paul can rejoice in all things, see death as gain, press on to maturity, and stand firm because of the truth of these two verses. How do these verses motivate you to persevere and mature (and even have joy) in your walk with Christ?

Read "Pressing On to the Goal" on the next page for more application to this lesson.

Pressing On to the Goal

By Melanie Newton

The goals in Paul's life had changed over the course of his 60+ years of age. He stated emphatically that before he became a Christian, his goal was to be the best Jew—#1 Hebrew, CEO of the Pharisees. His course for reaching that goal was to study hard, practice the Law to achieve perfection, wipe out the Christians. He was highly successful in his endeavors and close to reaching his initial goals UNTIL something happened. He met Jesus in a blinding light on the road to Damascus. The goals of his life changed—not to be top dog Pharisee anymore but to be like Christ—to know Him, to understand the real impact of His resurrection, to share in HIs sufferings, to face death as purposefully as did Jesus, to be resurrected from the state of death and given a new, sinless body. All of this is Paul's new definition of perfection.

He knows he hasn't reached this goal yet although to everyone else around him he was a spiritual giant. It had been 30 years since he started this spiritual journey. If you study Paul's life as we did last year by studying Acts, you see that he had ups and downs, battles to face.

But Paul pursued Christlikeness with the enthusiasm and persistence of a runner in the Greek games. And that's the context of today's passage. Running the course. The Christian life is like running a marathon on a designated course. Are any of you runners now or have been in the past? Paul used the analogy of running a race in several of his writings. Let's look at them:

> *"Brothers I do not consider myself yet to have taken hold of it. But one thing I do: forgetting what is behind and straining toward what is ahead. I press on toward the goal to win the prize for which God has called me heavenward in Christ Jesus." (Phil 3:13-14)*

Paul's words in 1 Cor. 9:24-27 raises the questions of "How are we to run?" and "What is the prize?" The latter is mentioned in our Philippians passage. In 2 Timothy 4:7-8, Paul wrote about finishing the race—his race. Paul was aware of imminent death. He had kept the faith. We get a glimpse into the prize that was awaiting him, and us.

So what questions are we motivated into asking?

#1. What is the course?
#2. What is the finish?
#3. What is the purpose of running it?
#4. What gets us off the course?
#5. How do we stay on the course?
#6. What is the prize?

What is the course?

The course is your life as a believer. It is whatever personal course God has given you as a believer. It is different for each person and contains the idea of stewardship—managing the things from God placed in your care such as yourself, your marriage, your children, your money or lack of it, your possessions, your talents, your skills, and your vocal ability to communicate. The list goes on. Write down your list. Some of it may be what you are born with for which you can take no credit—your genetics. Being an American. Include spiritual gifts. You course to run includes all of this.

What is the finish?

Unlike a sprint, a marathon is a race of endurance. The goal is not usually in sight but can be visualized. You know it is there. Most marathoners run not with the idea of winning the race but just to finish it. The finish line for the believer is our physical death. Paul said he has finished the race because he knew he would die soon. Throughout Philippians, we have seen that he was ready to face physical death and pass from death into life with Jesus. He reminds us that our citizenship is in heaven not here on earth and that we should all be eagerly awaiting our Savior's coming for us.

What is the purpose of running this race?

The purpose of running the race is to become more like Jesus—the only true perfection. And the way we run this race is by keeping the faith. God doesn't measure our faithfulness in pure bottom-line numbers. We need to be faithful in whatever He gives us. We are here on earth although our citizenship is in heaven. While here, we are to be living a life of faith—daily.

What gets us off the course?

False teaching, not spending time in prayer and Bible reading, emotional drains, difficult circumstances and people—all these can get us off the course. Life is not static. One thing I've learned is not to count on next year being like this year or the past one. As we mature physically, our bodies change; so do our emotions, priorities, and aspirations. What you consider to be important in your 20's is replaced by other attitudes and needs in your 30's and 40's.

Self-pity gets us off the course. Taking our eyes off Jesus and what we have in Him. Little irritations. Bad counsel. Lack of discernment. Being caught up in the materialism of our society. Not knowing the truth so we get swayed by every philosophy that comes our way. The past—regretting past mistakes. I wallow in past regrets at times. Because I have a tendency to be a perfectionist.

Any perfectionist tendencies in here? That tendency ruled my life for 19 years. Like Paul, I pursued the highest standards of behavior, achievements, and awards, just for the thrill of being the best. 4.0 in high school, cried if I made a B. Won awards in many areas. Felt I had to be perfect to win the approval of my parents and God. Then I met Jesus.

For the first time in my life, I didn't have to be perfect anymore. My grades slipped as I spent more time in Bible Study and discipleship. I began the race. I began pursuing Christlikeness. And like Paul, I counted those former achievements and the previous goal of my life to be rubbish in comparison to the love, joy, and peace I finally came to know in Christ. I saw that my character was sinful. An infinite number of awards and achievements could never make up for it. The greatest burden lifted from my shoulders was finding out I didn't have to be perfect to please God. Jesus already did that for me. Now, I wanted to be like Jesus—I was on the course, off and running. For many years now, I have been striving to keep the faith in whatever God has asked of me. I want to be the woman of God, not the woman of the world. I don't want to be described only by what I have done in my career, the eyes of the world.

Our circumstances have continually changed. We have been self-employed, worked for the government, worked in Christian ministry, lived on missionary support, or lived on no income at all. We have lived in places we've loved and places we hated. Our parents have gone through illness and death. At times, we were both content; other times, one of us has been very discontented about life. Yet the overall resolve of my life is to keep the faith—to know Him—to become like Christ.

How do we stay on course?

Be faithful. We have learned from Philippians that the responsibility of working in our lives rests upon our shoulders alone. Right?? No! We have learned that it is God who is working in us. He started it, He is working now, and He will complete it. He does the working to make us Christlike because it gives Him pleasure. God knows what we're going through, he can get us through it and back on course if we only ask. We only need to respond to Him. We should make it our goal to know Him as Paul did. Recognize Christ in every area of our lives. This leads me to one of my favorite topics—truth. When I became a believer, I realized that all the knowledge I was striving for through academics was meaningless and could be detrimental to my Christian growth if it did not come from God. I heard Dr. Henry Brandt say that we have a tendency to take man's wisdom over God's wisdom on a daily basis without even knowing that we are doing it. He was talking about psychology—a very pagan, humanistic academic subject. A lot of people have been messed up by psychology that is not rooted in God's Word and His truth.

Truth is very important to me. After becoming a believer, I desired to know God's truth on every subject—science, history, and literature. I determined early on that our children should not waste their minds learning rubbish from a secular view point that totally leaves out God but should learn all truth from the viewpoint of God's intimate dealings with mankind. To study from the Christian world view not the secular worldview. Not glorifying man but recognizing God's dealings with man throughout history and man's response to God. That's what history really is. God's dealings with man, man's response to God, and the consequences of those responses. The Scripture continually refers to history as a teaching tool—see what God did, see how the Jews responded and the consequences, see what God does for the Jews again, see how they respond.

Consider God's Word faithful, test it out. You will not be disappointed.

What is the prize?

The prize is given to everyone crossing the goal line. This is not about salvation here. It is the pursuit of knowing Christ, of being faithful. We don't know what the prizes are but we do know they will be good because they'll be given by a good God. Shall my prize be "Well done thou good and faithful servant" from my heavenly king? Great!! That would be enough.

Rewards are usually mentioned in scripture in the context of either persecution or a long hard time of service that goes unrecognized. Paul mentioned a crown of righteousness in 2 Timothy. Not only for him, but also for all who have longed for his appearing—the faithful ones. In 1 Corinthians9, Paul tells us that our reward will be a crown that will last forever. We also see the same thing in I Peter 1. Imperishable, undefiled, will not fade away, reserved in heaven for you.

We are not responsible for the prize—that's God—He determines what is given to each believer. We are responsible for running the course, staying true to the course and being faithful all the way to the time when we cross the finish line. We are not in competition with anyone else. It is our own personal course.

Our being in heaven would be reward enough. But for the time being, Paul exhorts the Philippians and us to live up to what we already have—a righteous position in Christ. He exhorts us to forget the past and stretch forward to the future as a runner leaning forward to reach that goal. What goal? Knowing Christ and being like Him How? By following the upward call which is our own personal course to run. And the prize will be there when we cross the finish line—physical death—after which we experience spiritual eternity, bliss, joy, and contentment... Now, we want to glorify God—do what He has created me to do on earth. Then we will enjoy Him forever—that's doing what He created us for then!

Lesson Ten: Joy—Firm Yet Gentle

Philippians 4:1-5

1. Read Philippians 4:1-5. Notice ALL the affectionate terms Paul uses to describe the Philippians! Re-read verse one. *Therefore,* this means that because of what was just said, now we need to do something, in this case "stand firm in the Lord." Review Paul's initial exhortation in 1:27-28 (first part). In *what* were they to "stand firm"?

2. Paul instructed the Philippians on *how* and *why* to "stand firm in the Lord" in Philippians 1:27-3:21. Review the following verses and summarize Paul's instructions to the Philippians (and to us) on *how* and *why* to stand firm: *Being in one spirit* (especially 2:1-8, 14-15)

    - How?

    - Why?

3. Not being alarmed by opponents (especially Philippians 3:12-14, 17, 20-21; 2:9-11)

    - How?

    - Why?

4. What were the chief obstacles to standing firm? Review Philippians 2:3-4, 14-15; 3:2-3, 15-19.

5. Earlier in this letter to the Philippians Paul had mentioned the examples of two men besides Jesus and himself who had already modeled this "standing firm". Name them.

Focus on the Meaning: Standing firm means steadfastly resisting the negative influences of temptation, false teaching, or persecution. To stand firm requires perseverance when we are challenged or opposed—With the Holy Spirit's help and with the help of fellow believers, we can stand firm in the Lord. (*Life Application Bible Commentary*, p. 108)

Paul's usual style whenever he addressed a problem or "sticky" issue was to first teach through the truth that applied, then address the specific concern in the church. Re-read Philippians 4:2-3. Women were significant in the founding of the Philippian church as well as other churches. Paul greatly esteemed his female co-laborers in the Lord as seen in Romans 16:1-3, 6, 12-15. Review Acts 16:11-15, 40 to see how the Philippian church was started. The letter to the Philippians was written 10-11 years later.

6. Paul speaks directly to two women here in Philippians 4:2-3. Paul asks them to do what he taught in 2:2. What was it?

7. Apply what you learned concerning "standing firm" in the previous questions to the apparent breach of relationship between these two women. How would standing firm in the Lord help the existing conflict and benefit the church as a whole?

8. As long as there are fallible humans on this earth, there will be relationship challenges. No church is immune to this. Read James 4:1-3. What are we told about potential sources of conflict for believers?

9. Read Philippians 4:3 again. Notice the request Paul makes of a "loyal yokefellow (NIV)/true comrade (NAS)." What responsibility does the local church body have (individually or as a whole) to encourage reconciliation of any of its members? Read also John 15:12-13, 17; Galatians 6:1-2 and Ephesians 4:14-16.

Scriptural Insight: The Book of Life, first mentioned in the Old Testament (Exodus 32:32-33; Psalm 69:28; 139:16), referred to a register of all citizens in God's kingdom. The "book" symbolizes God's knowledge of who belong to Him. Ancient cities had roll books that contained the names of all who had a right to citizenship. Under the New Covenant, Christians are on God's register, and He will admit all on the roll into heaven (Philippians 3:20). ALL believers are guaranteed a listing in the Book of Life and will be introduced to the hosts of heaven as belonging to Christ (Luke 10:17-20; Hebrews 12:22-23; Revelation 3:5; 20:11-15.) No believer will be forgotten, for the names are listed for eternity. (Adapted from *NIV Study Bible*, p. 1948; *Life Application Bible Commentary*, p. 112)

10. ***Your Joy Journey:***

    - How can Paul's admonition in Philippians 4:2-3 help you in your own relationships within the church?

    - Should you experience a problem relationship, how best can you respond when others attempt to counsel you? (See also Proverbs 12:1; 13:10; 19:20.)

    Think About It: Oh, beloved, pray! Pray that **you** may not be the cause of any disruptions in your church, that **you** may not be a part of hindering the work of the church for the cause of Christ! And pray to follow in Paul's wise footsteps if you must ever be a part of helping to solve a dispute between others. (Elizabeth George, *Experiencing God's Peace*, p. 111)

11. Read Philippians 4:4-5. Once again (see also 3:1), in verse 4, we are reminded of the attitude that is to be the response of all believers.

    - What is it?
    - Why can we do this? Support your answer with other verses from Philippians.

12. Paul sums up the principles he has been teaching in his letter thus far in this one word: *gentleness*. Review what you have learned in this lesson, then describe what Paul means when he says, "Let your gentleness be evident to all."

> ***Focus on the Meanings:*** *Joy*, an inner quality in relation to circumstances, may not always be seen; but the way one reacts to others, whether in gentleness or harshness, will be noticed. In Philippians 4:5, Paul exhorts the Philippians, and us, to let our gentleness (NIV)/ forbearing spirit (NAS) be evident to all. *Gentleness* is joy outwardly expressed. The Greek word for gentleness is a difficult word to fully translate in English. It refers to a spirit that is reasonable, fair-minded, and charitable; willing to yield one's own rights to show consideration to others but without sacrificing truth; non-retaliatory. One synonym is graciousness. Jesus never sacrificed truth in order to be gentle, but He always had a gentle spirit that often disarmed those set against Him. (*The Bible Knowledge Commentary NT*, p.663)

13. In light of the expected return of Christ ("the Lord is near"), why let your gentleness be evident to all? For help, review Philippians 1:10, 27; 2:15-16; 3:20-21; 4:5.

> *Read "Serving One Another Through Conflict" on the next page for more application to this lesson.*

Serving One Another through Conflict

By Melanie Newton

Picture this. The city is surrounded by enemy soldiers. The young king and his officials inside the city walls stubbornly refuse to leave, saying, "We won't lose. We won't give up our special city. " One voice, however, kept giving them the real news. "You won't win. God has given this city to Nebuchadnezzar. The people will die of starvation and disease. The city will be burned. Your family will be destroyed unless you surrender." The king is Zedekiah, the lone voice is God's prophet, Jeremiah. The rest of the story is in Jeremiah 38:14-28. Zedekiah's response was not to accept God's mercy and grace through obeying Him, doing it His way. Instead, Zedekiah chose to protect himself and listen to his peers, to ignore the conflict and hope it goes away. It didn't. Zedekiah's entire family was killed; he was blinded and held in chains.

CONFLICT IS NORMAL

Conflict. The word has a distasteful overtone. But, because we are human and sin still dwells within us, because we still live in this fallen world, conflict is an everyday part of life. Having or not having conflict isn't the issue. For believers, it's what we do when we are faced with conflict. That's the issue.

Having enemies surrounding your city wall is outside pressure. In the scriptures, Paul referred to those outside pressures that affect us individually and our church—persecutions, enemies, false teachers, and the Roman authorities. He addressed those pressures. *Stand firm in one spirit. Do not be afraid.* But, those outside pressures often cause friction to develop within. You know that pressure on your husband from his job will affect your relationship as a couple. Soon you have your own interpersonal conflict. That's what appears to be going on in Philippi.

In our previous study of Philippians 2:1-11, we saw Jesus, fully God and fully man, as the ultimate servant and our example for service. We are to serve Jesus through serving one another as He did. I shared with you four aspects of being a joyful servant:

- Thinking of others before yourself.
- Serving wholeheartedly.
- Sacrificing willingly without whining.
- Glorifying God as walking, talking visible representatives of the invisible God.

We serve Jesus together, and we serve one another individually. Part of Serving Jesus through serving one another is resolving interpersonal conflict within the Body. Conflict wounds His body and minimizes the effectiveness of the church to advance the gospel. It's hard to preach Christ and make disciples when we are spending emotional energy on internal conflict. Right? Interpersonal conflict can take many forms from simple behavior clashes (two women who just don't blend well together) to open defiance of one another. Regardless of the form, a conflict presents opportunity for growth. In fact, some people don't pay attention to their needs for growth in an area of their lives until conflict occurs.

RESOLVING INTERPERSONAL CONFLICT GOD'S WAY

In today's passage, Philippians 4:3-4, we don't know anything about these women. Perhaps they were two of the women at the river who first received the gospel from Paul. Maybe they were deaconesses in the church. It is sad that these two women have become the brunt of jokes. Paul calls them fellow workers for the gospel. They weren't bimbos. They weren't insignificant troublemakers. They were laborers in the spread of the gospel at Philippi. These were probably mature women, well known by the recipients of the letter. For our purposes today, we will call them Elizabeth and Cindy.

We don't know what their conflict was. One commentator said, "It may have been accidental friction between two energetic Christian women." Perhaps they took turns having the church at each other's home. Elizabeth may have criticized what Cindy did when she hosted everybody. Not enough food. The chairs were too close together. Perhaps Cindy dared to discipline Elizabeth's child. That's all it takes. Whatever happened affected the unity of the congregation. It was brought to Paul's attention. This was a wound in the Philippians body. Apparently ineffective means had been used to stop the bleeding. Paul speaks directly to this situation in his letter, and from his wise advice, we can draw three principles regarding conflict resolution.

THE PRINCIPLES

Principle #1: "In the Lord"

The church is a living organism, not an organization. An organism made of individual parts. Just as our human bodies respond immediately to repair a wound whether minor or major, so should the body of Christ. Suppose you cut your finger. What happens? The body does whatever it takes to enable the healing process to take place. The closest cells start working to clot the blood, close the wound with a scab, and fight invading germs. It is the responsibility of those cells closest to the wound to get there first and stop the bleeding. Then, others step in to help repair the damage and make the body stronger. So also within the body of Christ. The cells within our physical body know what to do. The members of Christ's body don't always know what to do. But, the Word gives us direction and guidance so that we can be obedient.

I don't seek opportunities to resolve conflicts. Most of the time, my response is to ignore the seeds of conflict, hoping that by ignoring it, the tension will be smoothed over and just go away. I want everyone to be part of a team and to get along as a team. Another excuse of mine: I don't think quickly on my feet. So, how can the Lord use me to manage any kind of crisis between two people when I can't think straight? Actually, He doesn't want me to manage it at all. He wants me to allow Him to do His work through me. I have to be weak so He can be strong through me. He wants my obedience. The cells in the elbow have to be just as ready to repair a wound as the cells in the finger or the heart. Ready to function as designed, dependent on the lifeblood to bring the ingredients necessary to heal the wound. The purpose of the action is to promote healing.

Principle #2: Agree with each other (or, live in harmony).

This is one-on-one. As soon as you recognize that you are in a conflict with a sister, then you are responsible to do something. Agree to work on it. That's Obedience. Give up your rights to be right. That's humility. The reason is for the good of the relationship and for the church family. This is another aspect of serving one another as Jesus did.

Speaking of Jesus, what did He teach about this?

- Matthew 5:23-24 — You know your sister has something against you; you have offended her, go to her and be reconciled to her.
- Matthew 18:15-17 — Your sister has offended you, go to her alone, tell her what she has done. If she listens, you will be reconciled.

Paul gives us more info on how to be reconciled.

- Ephesians 4:15-16 — speak truth in love for the building up and growing of the body, out of love for her and the Body. That's your motivation.

- Ephesians 4:32 — heart attitude

Did you notice Jesus' emphasis on confidentiality and trust? First, go alone. Go directly to the person with whom you are in conflict. Then, just a few carefully selected individuals, then the authority over that person. Notice, Jesus did not say to talk about it to anyone who'll listen. Sometimes you can seek counsel from a trusted friend on how to proceed. However, it's easy to cross the line to complaining and gossiping. I call it **sharing sensitive information in inappropriate settings**. It's sensitive because anything negative said about a person or a ministry plants seeds of doubt in the other woman's mind about that person or the ministry as a whole. That is not beneficial to the body. Someone always gets hurt. It's an inappropriate setting when that person you are telling has no oversight or authority to do something about the situation.

For a ministry, go to the person involved in the decision-making process for that ministry. Chances are she is fully aware of the challenge. Your solution may have already been tried. Or, the timing isn't right yet. Whatever, the hardest part is leaving it there. Isn't it? Trust. That's what is involved in being humble. Serving Jesus through serving one another in love, not hurting anyone or the Body as a whole.

Principle #3: Help them— Intervention.

Paul urges others around the two women to help them come together. That is our responsibility. Why? A body works to repair itself so it can function effectively. What do you do when two of your friends are bickering with each other? For our purposes, let's talk about two stages of conflict: 1) Developing and 2) Situational.

Developing means that over a period of time, the relationship between two women is gradually creating more friction. Their friends may recognize clues that this is happening, and someone who cares speaks the truth in love to both parties in hopes of heading off an explosion perhaps by way of a phone call or a chat over lunch. Ideally, this is the most fruitful stage to help two women become reconciled. It's like a paper cut that hurts but heals quickly.

Ignoring those opportunities usually brings about an emotional crisis situation. That's called a **situational** conflict. What has built up is now brought to a head by a wrong word, look, or a sudden change of plans. A crisis exists. Something has to be done to help them immediately. Women in crisis conflict have suddenly lost perspective; they feel like they have been turned upside down. That's why it presents a tremendous opportunity for personal growth. But, they need an unbiased third party who loves them enough to intercede and help them talk it out. This is called Crisis Intervention.

Okay, when do you intervene?

1. When the two women have not been able to resolve their differences on their own. Jesus said, "You are responsible to go to the one who offended you or the one you offended and be reconciled to her." If that hasn't been tried, suggest it. If it has been tried but hasn't worked, then outside help is needed.

2. When the conflict endangers the safety or welfare of the body of Christ. You can give them perspective and help them to focus on the greater good. That's what Paul did.

3. When there is an emotional explosion, help immediately.

What are the A-B-Cs of conflict resolution?

A = Achieve Trusting Contact with each Conflicting Party.

In other words, get their attention. Ideally, this should be separately with each one. First talk to the one most agitated then to the calmest. Don't let them vent on each other or on you. You are the unbiased party. How do you achieve trusting contact? Through a setting that is private and undisturbed where confidentiality can be preserved. Be relaxed and genuinely kind and concerned. Listen carefully but objectively by asking questions such as "What happened?" Collect the facts. Let the pauses come. It's not your time to talk. Listen carefully.

B = Boil Down What the Presenting Problems Are (Simplify the Issue).

To do this, use reflective listening skills. Concentrate on responding and focusing. Responding is to feed back her own words but in the form of clarifying questions such as *"Are you telling me...?", "Did I hear you say...?", "What I am hearing you say is...?"* This guarantees to the person that you understand. Focusing means to help the women make conclusions as to the real presenting problems that they face. Collect the facts related to the crisis only. Not every problem she has experienced over the past year. Separate the issues. What actually caused the conflict—THIS TIME. One or two actual things that are causing the immediate conflict.

C = Cope Actively (Make A Way Out, A Plan).

Help by providing a way out of the conflict. Establish goals that are possible, measurable, and short-term. Tactfully suggest some non-threatening options:

- What do you want to see happen?
- What can I do to help you out?
- How would you see the plan carried out? "What will you do? How will you do it? By when will you do this?"
- How are we going to evaluate this later on? Be willing to follow-up and ask, "How is it working?" "What do you need to change in the plan if anything?"

You might have them pray for each other's needs. Perhaps arrange short, periodic meetings between them for sharing. If they are co-workers, develop clear job descriptions so that each will know what she is to do and not do. Talk about how to warn each other about possible conflict in a non-explosive way.

Conclusion

We are one in the Lord who has one Body. Any cut, tear, or break causes the Body pain and negatively affects the advance of the gospel. We are Christ's, not the world's. We are to behave differently because we think differently about one another. We are to be obedient. Not like Zedekiah who could have saved his family and the city had he obeyed. God's ways are not our ways. They are tons better.

> Oh, beloved, pray! Pray that **you** may not be the cause of any disruptions in your church, that **you** may not be a part of hindering the work of the church for the cause of Christ! And pray to follow in Paul's wise footsteps if **you** must ever be a part of helping to solve a dispute between others. (Elizabeth George, *Experiencing God's Peace*, page 111)

Lesson Eleven: Joyful Thinking

Philippians 4:6-9

What's worry? The Greek word translated "anxious" in verse 6 means "to be pulled in different directions." ...Worry is the greatest thief of joy. It is not enough for us, however, to tell ourselves to "quit worrying," because that will never capture the thief. Worry is an "inside job," and it takes more than good intentions to get the victory. The antidote to worry is the secure mind. (Warren Wiersbe, *Be Joyful*, pp. 125-126)

1. Read Philippians 4:6-9. What do you see in Philippians 4:7 that could cause you not to have joy?

2. What does Paul tell the Philippians, and you, to do about this potential joy-stealer?

3. What should be our attitude in prayer? Why is this attitude important?

> ***Focus on the Meanings:*** The word for **prayer** is a general term meaning worshipful conversation with God, while **petition (supplication)** refers to a prayer with a sense of need. **Thanksgiving** focuses on the attitude of one's heart in approaching God. **Requests** refers to directly asking God's help regarding specific needs. (*Life Application Bible Commentary, Philippians, Colossians & Philemon*, p. 115)

4. Read Matthew 6:25-34.

    - What does Jesus say in this passage about worry?

    - What does this passage reveal about God?

    - What does Jesus say to do (verse 33), and what does this mean (how can you do this)?

5. The result is a promise! Let's take Philippians 4:7 apart and examine each phrase individually. Observe and define what each phrase means (use a dictionary as necessary):

   a. **The peace of God**
      - Isaiah 26:3, 12 –

      - John 14:27 –

      - John 16:33 –

   b. **Transcends (surpasses) all understanding (comprehension)**
      - Psalm 147:5 –

      - Isaiah 55:8-9 –

   c. **Guard your hearts and minds in Christ Jesus** (There is only 1 other instance of the word "guard" used similarly in the New Testament. In 1 Peter 1:5 it is used to mean we are secure in salvation through Him.)

      Focus on the Meaning: The Greek word for "guard" is a military term that means to surround and protect a garrison or city. The Philippians, living in a garrison town, were familiar with the Roman guards who maintained watch, guarding the city from any outside attack. (*Life Application Bible Commentary, Philippians, Colossians & Philemon*, p. 116)

6. *Your Joy Journey:* Summarize in your own words the truths learned above and record what Philippians 4:7 means to *you*. Feel free to use any creative means to describe this (drawing, poem, song, other).

Think About It: Every time we pray, our horizon is altered, our attitude to things is altered, not sometimes but every time, and the amazing thing is that we don't pray more. (Oswald Chambers (1874-1917))

7. **Your Joy Journey:** Paul knew that our pervading thoughts would determine our actions that would in turn reveal our heart attitude. In Philippians 4:8, Paul describes what should pervade a believer's thoughts. Are you currently worried about a difficult circumstance in your life? Can you think back to a time when you went through a difficult circumstance that caused you concern? You can work through your difficulty using verse 8 (and below) as a guide for rightful thinking. Select 3 or 4 principles and explain how "thinking on these things" can help you work through any difficulty. It might help to consider also the opposite to these.

   - Something true–

   - Something noble (honorable, worthy of respect)–

   - Something right (just)–

   - Something pure (wholesome)–

   - Something lovely–

   - Something admirable (of good repute, commendable)–

   - Something excellent (virtuous)–

   - Something praiseworthy–

8. Why is it so important for us to focus our minds on true and excellent things? See also 2 Corinthians 10:4-5 and Colossians 3:1-3.

9. **Your Joy Journey:** What could you meditate and think upon that would most definitely measure up to all of Paul's criteria? Consider how you might apply these guidelines in verse 8 to your day-to-day choices (TV, books, radio, other). Share your insights with your small group to encourage one another to right thinking.

10. Paul gives us a simple formula for joyful thinking in Philippians 4:8-9. Fill in the blanks to see what that formula is.

- Philippians 4:8 tells us what to _____.

- Philippians 4:9 tells us what to _____.

- Philippians 4:9 tells us what the result will be: _____.

11. **Your Joy Journey:** What have you learned from this passage in Philippians about the connection between practicing right thinking and knowing joy in your life?

Lesson Twelve: Joyful Living and Giving

Philippians 4:10-23

Read Philippians 4:10-23.

1. Slowly re-read Philippians 4:10-13. What caused Paul to rejoice?

2. Describe the overall tone of this passage.

3. In verse 12 Paul uses several pairs of opposites to describe what he has learned. List the pairs here.

> ***Scriptural Insight:*** Paul makes an interesting comment in verse 12 about living in prosperity. How can he say this? Paul knew firsthand about wealth and privileges that come with being a prominent Pharisee in the Jewish community and also of being a Roman citizen (Acts 22:3-5, 25-29; 26:4-5).

4. What secret had Paul learned and how had he learned it?

> ***Focus on the Meaning:*** The word *content* in Greek means "self-sufficient" and independent of others. Paul used this term to indicate his independence of everything but Christ, since Christ was the sole source of Paul's life (Philippians 1:21, 4:13). This contrasted with the Stoic philosophy (of the day) that used the word "content" to describe a person who impassively accepted whatever came. A Stoic view fostered self-sufficiency to the point that all the resources for coping with life came from within oneself. Paul explained that his sufficiency was in Christ alone, who provides strength to cope with all circumstances. (*Life Application Commentary, Philippians*, p. 121)

5. What do Paul's words teach you about contentment?

6. The Greek term for "learned" is used only here in the New Testament. It was an expression used to describe an initiation by experience. What kind of experiences had Paul had? Read the following passages and record your findings.

    - 1 Corinthians 4:11-13—

    - 2 Corinthians 11:23-29—

7. How could Paul, a prisoner and one who had experienced so many difficulties, possibly be content? See the following passages for hints.

    - 2 Corinthians 4:7-10—

    - 2 Corinthians 4:16-18—

    - 2 Corinthians 12:8-10 –

8. *Your Joy Journey:* In what circumstances do you struggle with being content? Why do you suppose it is such a struggle?

9. Read Habakkuk 3:17-18. What decision did Habakkuk make?

10. ***Your Joy Journey:*** What decisions can you make now so that you are prepared to endure those times of struggle?

> ***Think About It:*** All of nature depends on hidden resources. The great trees send their roots down into the earth to draw up water and minerals. Rivers have their sources in the snow-capped mountains. The most important part of a tree is the part you cannot see, the root system, and the most important part of the Christian's life is the part that only God sees. Unless we draw upon the deep resources of God by faith, we fail against the pressures of life. Paul depended on the power of Christ at work in his life. "I can through Christ!" was Paul's motto, and it can be our motto, too. (Warren Wiersbe, *Be Joyful*, p. 137)

11. Re-read Philippians 4:14-19. What do we learn about the Philippian church, and what characteristics do its members demonstrate in this passage?

Paul didn't always accept aid. In 1 Corinthians 9:11-19 Paul wrote that he had not accepted money from the Corinthian church in order to avoid being accused of preaching only to get money (preaching for the wrong reasons). In fact, while he was in Corinth, the Philippian believers helped him (2 Corinthians 11:9). He accepted their offering because they gave it willingly in order to help Paul.

12. In Philippians 4:17 Paul writes that he is not looking for more "gifts" from the Philippians. Instead he likens their gifts to investments credited to an account. What does he mean by this metaphor? See the following verses for help with your answer.

    - Matthew 6:19-21—

    - Hebrews 6:10—

    - Revelation 22:12—

13. Paul calls their gifts a "sacrifice…to God" (verse 18). In what sense was their gift an offering to God? (See also Hosea 6:6, Hebrews 13:15-16, Ephesians 5:2 for hints.)

> ***Scriptural Insight:*** The priest in the Old Testament went into the holy place to put incense on the altar and it ascended with a sweet smell. A Christian in his giving is like a priest making an offering to God—see Leviticus 7:12-15. (J. Vernon McGee, *Through the Bible Commentary, Philippians*, p. 105)

14. The Philippian church was not wealthy (see 2 Corinthians 8:1-4), though they gave with a heart of generosity. What does Paul tell them in Philippians 4:19?

15. What is the connection between the first part of today's passage on contentment with the last part regarding giving?

16. **Your Joy Journey:** From your study of this passage and the entire letter to the Philippians:

    - What interferes with your believing that God will meet all of your needs? (List them here and **replace them**!)

    - What helps you believe that God will meet all of your needs? (List them here and refer to them when you need help!)

Joy in Summary

"...And this is my prayer: that your love may abound more and more in knowledge and depth of insight, so that you may be able to discern what is best and may be pure and blameless until the day of Christ, filled with the fruit of righteousness that comes through Jesus Christ—to the glory and praise of God...Rejoice in the Lord always. I will say it again: Rejoice!" (Philippians 1:9-11, 4:4)

17. **Your Joy Journey:** Take a few minutes and look back over your study through Philippians. Think about the truths you know about Jesus, or about your relationship with Jesus, that bring joy to your heart. Use a creative medium (song, poem, prayer, drawing, craft, other) to illustrate this on the next page.

LESSON TWELVE

Sources

1. Carol Kent, *Becoming A Woman of Influence*
2. Cynthia Heald, *Becoming A Woman of Grace*
3. Elizabeth George, *Experiencing God's Peace*
4. J. Vernon McGee, *Through the Bible Commentary, Philippians*
5. *Life Application Commentary, Philippians, Colossians & Philemon*
6. *NIV Study Bible*
7. Oswald Chambers, *My Utmost for His Highest*
8. The Teachers Commentary
9. Walvoord and Zuck, *The Bible Knowledge Commentary New Testament*
10. Warren Wiersbe, *Be Joyful*

Graceful Beginnings Series
FOR NEW-TO-THE-BIBLE CHRISTIANS

Designed for anyone new to the Bible. First steps for new Christians. Basic lessons introducing truths about God. Simple terms that are easily understood. Where you can start studying the Bible for yourself.

A Fresh Start

The first book in the series, laying a good foundation of truth for you to grasp and apply to your life.

Painting the Portrait of Jesus

Study the "I Am" statements of Jesus from the gospel of John that reveal who Jesus is and why you can trust Him.

The God You Can Know

Study the wonderful attributes of God so you can know Him as your loving Father.

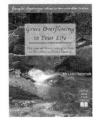

Grace Overflowing

An overview of Paul's letters and how Christ is presented in each one as the answer to your every need.

For more information about *Graceful Beginnings* books, including new releases, visit **www.joyfulwalkpress.com**.

Made in the USA
Middletown, DE
20 August 2019